What people are saying about …

GRACE BOMB

"Simple. Inspiring. Contagious. Essential. That's Grace Bomb. As followers of Jesus, we know we are *objects* of His grace. Yet we fall short of being *instruments* of His grace toward others. That's where Pat Linnell mentors us through a neighbor-loving explosion of grace bombing that can change you, your neighbor, and the nations!"

Greg St. Cyr, DMin, lead pastor of Bay Area
Community Church, Annapolis, MD

"Pat Linnell has done something remarkable in capturing the stories of what it looks likes to be a conduit of grace. He not only gives a deep theological basis for why we should be people of grace but provides the inspiration of how grace changes lives, as Jesus intended it to do so. *Grace Bomb* restores your hope in the church and sounds the alarm for a new day."

Sammy Foster, lead pastor of Lighthouse
Church, author of *Elements: Four
Priorities of the Modern Day Disciple*

"What's better than random acts of kindness? Intentional acts of kindness prompted by the Holy Spirit. *Grace Bomb* is pure delight from start to finish and will give you that spark you need to jump into the adventure of faith, doing those good works prepared in advance for you to do.... This is a movement we can all get behind. A movement of love and grace, and we were made for it."

Tracey Tiernan, radio host 95.1 SHINE-FM,
"Your Day Brighter" podcast

"Three words stand out frequently in this magnificent work: *taking Jesus seriously*! With disarming vulnerability and practical application models, *Grace Bomb* invites you to a lifestyle of loving your neighbor in obedience to Christ.... This is a must-read for church leaders and followers of Christ, and yet-to-be-followers of Christ will find here meaning and significance beyond their naturally inclined gestures of kindness and generosity. Highly recommended!"

The Rev. Dr. Casely Baiden Essamuah,
secretary of Global Christian Forum

"I remember when Pat came into my office to talk about *Grace Bomb*. I had recently taught our staff how to share their faith, and we were doing some evangelism training for the entire church as well. Those were exciting days. Pat asked me to read it, and I was truly astonished by its clarity, simplicity, and heart. LOVED IT. I am very critical of books by nature, but WOW was this just fabulous.... Now I am planning to use *Grace Bomb* as a class for all newcomers to Shelter Cove here in Modesto. Bravo, Pat. I am truly proud of you."

Edward F. Kelley IV, ThB, MMin, MTS,
executive pastor and management consultant

"Loving your neighbor is a truth that transcends countries and cultures and shows the world that Jesus Christ is real and changes lives. It is so refreshing to read a book that stirs my heart in new ways to make God's precious Word practical. In *Grace Bomb*, Pat Linnell has done just that. I am convinced if we all follow his suggestions for simply loving people, we will see a huge step toward building unity in our communities and pointing people to Jesus."

Dr. Robert Morrison McAlister, Global Catalyst

"*Grace Bomb* is a delightful and inspiring read. Pat writes in such a winsome, humorous, and practical fashion. The stories he shares pack some serious punch and emotion. On more than one occasion I fought back tears. Christians everywhere will feel inspired and equipped to bring the loving grace of Jesus by reading this book. Well done! I can't wait to get this into the hands of pastors and churches across the country!"

Buck Rogers, president of Empower Clarity, Inc.

"*Grace Bomb* is one of those books that has the potential to change the landscape of how people meet Jesus. I can't think of a better book for what the world needs right now. *Grace Bomb* illustrates how the smallest acts of grace can have the biggest impact on a person's spiritual life. Pat does a masterful job blending his personal and gritty look at the world with solid biblical truth and practical steps to loving people. You'll walk away inspired, prepared, and eager to live this out."

Brian Hopper, pastor, equipper, coach,
Bay Area Community Church

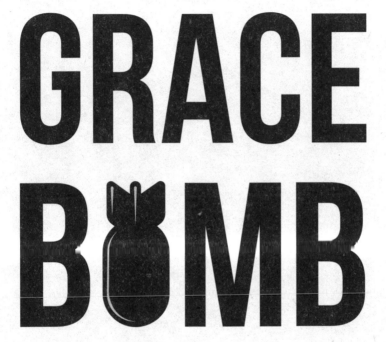

GRACE

THE SURPRISING IMPACT OF LOVING YOUR NEIGHBORS

PATRICK LINNELL

BMB

DAVID **C** COOK

transforming lives together

GRACE BOMB
Published by David C Cook
4050 Lee Vance Drive
Colorado Springs, CO 80918 U.S.A.

Integrity Music Limited, a Division of David C Cook
Brighton, East Sussex BN1 2RE, England

The graphic circle C logo is a registered trademark of David C Cook.

The website addresses recommended throughout this book are offered as a
resource to you. These websites are not intended in any way to be or imply an
endorsement on the part of David C Cook, nor do we vouch for their content.

Details in some stories have been changed to protect
the identities of the persons involved.

Unless otherwise noted, all Scripture quotations are taken from the ESV® Bible
(The Holy Bible, English Standard Version®), copyright © 2001 by Crossway, a
publishing ministry of Good News Publishers. Used by permission. All rights
reserved. Scripture quotations marked NIV are taken from THE HOLY BIBLE,
NEW INTERNATIONAL VERSION®, NIV® Copyright © 1973, 1978, 1984,
2011 by Biblica, Inc.® Used by permission. All rights reserved worldwide. Scripture
quotations marked BSB are taken from The Holy Bible, Berean Study Bible, BSB
Copyright © 2016, 2020 by Bible Hub. Used by Permission. All Rights Reserved
Worldwide. The author has added italics to Scripture quotations for emphasis.

Library of Congress Control Number 2020951238
ISBN 978-0-8307-8200-0
eISBN 978-0-8307-8201-7

The Team: Michael Covington, Kevin Scott, Megan Stengel,
Jack Campbell, Jon Middel, Susan Murdock
Cover Design: Meredith Thompson
Cover Photo of Author: Josh Shirlen

Printed in the United States of America
First Edition 2021

1 2 3 4 5 6 7 8 9 10

021821

To Ava, Jackson, Scarlett, and Max.

Contents

Acknowledgments

This book is by no means a solo project. It is a result of the faith steps of many others who, knowingly or not, helped bring into reality what you have in your hands. I am thankful to God for these souls whose labor for Jesus has shaped me and this work.

In the summer of 2014, from the back of a motorcycle, my bride, Kristen, spoke a vision for a movement. While I had been planning a book to trace God's grace throughout the Bible, she shouted above the wind about a book that was more than a book. It would be the genesis of a rapidly spreading movement, equipping and empowering people to demonstrate grace to others in a meaningful way. She envisioned real people caught up in giving real grace. I couldn't see it at the time, but a few years later, that idea became a reality in Grace Bomb. Kristen, thank you for encouraging me to greater faith and freeing me up for weeks on end to write this book. Thanks for growing old with me.

We'd both like to say thank you to Brian and Suzi Hopper, who blazed a trail of faith and lovingly welcomed us to follow. If it hadn't been for this couple, my life would have looked completely different. Triad.

In the summer of 2017, my mentor, Greg St. Cyr, encouraged me to revisit the idea for the book and preach a Grace Bomb sermon series that would help jump-start my writing. That was genius. Thanks, Greg, for your wisdom, for sharing the pulpit with me for many years, and for your constant reminder that we are all missionaries.

The branding that spurred on the Grace Bomb movement was shaped by the creative talents of Josh Shirlen, Jake Williams, Josh Burgin, and Arianne Teeple—thank you guys for your love for Jesus, relentless pursuit of excellence, and brilliance in helping to bring ancient truths alive through art and culture.

To the congregation at BACC, you are home, and it was your Grace Bombing adventures that started the party. Keep up the good works God has prepared for you! And yes, there are some stick figures in this book.

Thank you also to Pastor Sammy and the fun crew at Lighthouse Church in Glen Burnie, who let us test-drive Grace Bomb outside the Bay Area for the first time—you guys rock!

To Nate Thacker—you made me believe that I could write a book that would be of value to the church, as you freely gave your time and expertise in guiding me into this process and helped me see that words have the ability to hug people.

Teresa Evenson at the WKJ agency, thanks for giving me a chance to share my heart with you about why Grace Bomb is a powerful discipleship tool. And to Darren Heater who, without even knowing it, made that connection possible.

To Michael Covington and the entire team at David C Cook, thank you for making me feel right at home and being the answer to the prayer of not just having a publisher, but having a partner to empower the saints to light up their everyday walks of life for Jesus.

Thanks, Mom and Dad, for letting me run wild while still planting seeds of faith. Look, Mom, it's Midnight in Baltimore.

To Kristen's parents: Dave, for your creative insights, and Karan, for your unending practical help and care. Matt, thank you for your depth charge.

Thanks also to Mickey, for loaning me the Raptor, and to the Larimers and Sherri for providing quiet places on the water to write; to Meredith Thompson, who kept my grammar in check; and to J-Mad, for your timely GIFs to spur me on to keep writing and to remember my quest. And to Jen, for the reminder that "it's all unfolding perfectly."

Finally, this book is only in your hands because of the Grace Bombers all across the country who have shared their stories to spur us all on to love and good works. Keep looking out and keep taking Jesus seriously every day.

Foreword

At the dawn of each new day there lies a pointed question before us, one that we rarely perceive and almost never answer. In his premier book *Grace Bomb*, Pat Linnell tells us we are like a child straddling a bike atop the hill ready to take the drop. The question is whether we will mount and ride or stay static—will we sit in our assigned seat, follow the current as we did the day before; or will we take an alternative path, one of adventure, risk, love in form?

For the last fifteen years, I have had a front-row seat in Pat's life, as a friend, fellow father to a young family, and his wingman on the ice. More than that, I have seen and experienced from him the very things he pens through the pages of this wonderful book—God's grace! Pat represents an emerging generation of Christian leaders with vision to catalyze and equip the people of Jesus in today's grace-starved landscape.

Pat says we are made to fly down the hill, and this book gives us wings as Pat pushes us into the drop—the wind that comes, the rush of what it means to be alive in Jesus takes form through these pages. *Grace Bomb* takes us on the wonderful journey down the hill with Jesus. Through endless personal stories, humor, '80s and '90s cultural references, and describing the biblical landscape, Pat puts a tool in our hands that transforms *"grace* into a verb."

As an artist and storyteller, Pat juxtaposes the images of destruction (bomb) and reconstruction (grace), letting the imagery spill out into the everyday stuff of life. What emerges is a movement of imperfect people living radically different, acting in small and large ways to extend the invitation from heaven to earth through their words and actions. But the stories don't always get tied up in a bow—be prepared to learn how God might disrupt your life in order to restore it, as He did with Pat. While we are ushered through the pages of stories within God's bigger unfolding story, we will find ourselves imagining what it might mean for our stories.

Grace Bomb is no "random act of kindness" campaign but a properly rooted recalling of what grace-fueled obedience in Jesus Christ looks like. Pat takes the early twenty-first-American-century-kindness movement, which often lacks in sustaining motivation, and implicates Jesus—giving us the substantial "why" behind the human condition's impulse to do good. It is in Jesus that our fears are found conquered, in Jesus that we find one who moves toward the marginalized and oppressed, in Jesus that we see one who lived on the outside so we might be brought near. And Pat reminds us it is in Jesus that we find the resource of love through His death on the cross that electrifies us to demonstrate every lesser act of grace we echo.

So be prepared to become that child standing atop the high hill, straddling your bike, and hold on. You have a decision to make as you open these pages—if you simply read this book, you will continue to find yourself imagining the wind of the drop. But if for some reason you should dare to put flesh to what Pat is proposing, beware: your life might never be the same. You might just find yourself flying down the hill with Jesus, catching the wind in your face and experiencing the ride of your life. As C. S. Lewis through Mr. Beaver said of Aslan (Jesus), "Who said anything about safe? 'Course he isn't safe. But he's good. He's the King, I tell you." *Grace Bomb* is not a safe book, but it is good and it is what we as Jesus followers are called to and be reminded of: to demonstrably love people in our everyday lives. In the wake of the events of 2020, through the deeply divided and grace-starved world we find ourselves in, may this book be good for you and, through the power of the Holy Spirit, prepare you as wind to the world, to take the drop.

Joey Tomassoni
Annapolis, MD, 2021

Prologue

I have very few vivid memories from being a seven-year-old, but I remember with great clarity the day I learned to ride a bike. There were no helmets, no pads, no parents, no training wheels—just a slightly older, slightly wilder neighborhood kid named Sean who was bold enough to show me the ropes, lend me his blue BMX bike, and ask, "Who's up for the ride?" The challenge was simple: get on, hang on, and pedal like crazy.

Sean pushed me from behind at full sprinter speed, and when he let go, I borrowed the balance from his initial push to quickly find my own. For the first time, I was pedaling on two wheels. It was pure joy, evidenced by a super cheesy smile cemented on my face.

Those first fifty wobbly yards of freedom ended abruptly, though, when I veered off into a prickly bush at the end of the sidewalk. Crashing didn't matter. I was smiling ear to ear—with my imagination racing—having discovered that I could have adventures on my own, any day I wanted to ride. Learning to brake would come later. I was learning how to fly.

You were made to fly, with the wind flowing through your hair, into all the purposes God has planned for you. You were meant for great adventures of faith. You probably don't need another book to tell you this. In fact, books can sometimes keep us in a posture of sitting instead of flying. But this book aims to be like that neighborhood kid who gives you a bike and a push to show you what adventures are possible in your everyday life.

Your faith adventures will come in all shapes and sizes— following sidewalks and trails, jumping curbs and ramps, and cruising smooth scenic back roads or dodging cars on busy city streets. They may carry you near or far; sometimes on smooth roads, other times rough; sometimes solo, other times among friends. These adventures are largely found beyond Sunday services and the cozy confines of church life, where taking Jesus seriously is often less popular and harder to live out.

I get church, have lived "going to church," and love the church, but I also know from experience that the majority of church people are missing out on the adventure of living out faith during the week, beyond the events and opportunities created by church leaders. It's one thing to hear the simple commands of Jesus, and it's a whole other thing to put those things into practice on Monday at work, Tuesday on the soccer sidelines, and on Friday night at the party.

Grace Bomb focuses on just one of Jesus' commands: to love your neighbor. This simple and ancient calling is perhaps the best known yet least practiced of Jesus' commands.

The reality is that it can be hard to break the ice with a neighbor. It takes effort to look beyond our immediate needs and concerns. It can be a stretch to put down our phones and pay attention to the other people in line. It can feel unnatural to reach into our communities outside of a sponsored event or service. It can feel unjust not to repay evil with evil. It can feel wobbly to be the church for your neighbor who has never set foot in a church building. And it can seem awkward to point people beyond kindness to the source of kindness.

All of these challenges create the resistance needed to grow and get stronger. Loving your neighbor, with no strings attached, strengthens your core spiritual muscles. It can prepare you for and propel you into following other life-giving commands of Jesus. And it often results in a cheesy smile of joy cemented on your heart.

Steadily following Jesus' command to love your neighbor will produce growth in many areas of your life. It will help you grow in your awareness of and proximity to people as well as your prayer life, discernment in hearing God's voice, generosity, verbalizing your faith, and ultimately carrying out your purpose as a light in the world. Wow, saying all of that out loud makes simply "going to church" seem so much easier.

I'm putting *Grace Bomb* in your hands as a tool that makes *grace* a verb. It's a way to help you break the ice with your neighbors and give you a full-sprint push with stories from my life, the Bible, and the movement across the country. This is both a *how-to* book and a *why* book. It is an invitation to recognize how receiving divine grace into your own life and giving surprising grace into others' lives can make all the difference.

Together we will explore how grace-built people were made to grace bomb people. We'll see that we have a supernatural fuel supply to draw from in this endeavor. We'll learn to recognize barriers to exercising our faith that need dismantling. And all along the way, we'll look to Jesus, who provides our ultimate example of dropping life-changing grace.

So consider me the slightly older, slightly wilder kid who is pushing his bike across the street toward you. With a crazy look in my eye, I want to offer you a new tool and push you into the adventure of faith that you were quite literally made for. You could refuse and return to the familiar and comfortable, which might spare you some crashes and scraped knees, but it might also prevent your soul from taking flight.

Who's up for the ride?

Part One

A New Tool

The Daddy-Daughter Date

Your simple step of faith today could change someone's life forever.

*Now to him who is able to do immeasurably more than all
we ask or imagine, according to his power that is at work
within us, to him be glory in the church and in Christ Jesus
throughout all generations, for ever and ever! Amen.*

Ephesians 3:20–21 (NIV)

"Dad, we should grace bomb somebody!"

With those six words, a seven-year-old girl sparked a seemingly random chain of events that proved to be divine appointments with explosive, life-changing impact.

It began on an altogether normal Wednesday, as I pulled into the driveway after a long day of work, and it would take me well over a year to find out all that God was up to. On that unusually warm fall day in Maryland, my giddy anticipation of plopping down on the couch for a much-needed nap was interrupted when my youngest daughter, Scarlett, bounced out to meet me at the car, nearly jumping through the driver-side window to ask for a "daddy-daughter date." She wanted quality time with me and was eager to get out on the town, meaning a trip to McDonald's, Chick-fil-A, or on the rarest of occasions, the mall.

Admittedly, Scarlett, being the baby girl of the family, has me wrapped around her little finger, and she had me at hello. We had to be quick, because all four kids would be going to Awana, a midweek Bible camp, at the church down the road later in the evening. After a brief check-in at home, we busted a move to McDonald's for a Happy Meal and a discussion of the highs and lows of life as a first grader. As we arrived, Scarlett enthusiastically shouted, "Dad, we should grace bomb somebody!"

Genesis of Grace Bomb

Let me take a moment to explain how *Grace Bomb* became a verb and why my daughter was so excited about grace bombing somebody.

I've taught from the Bible in church settings for the past fifteen years and, in so doing, have continually encountered the mega-theme of God's grace—His unmerited, unconditional love and favor toward people. This grace is unsettling, disruptive, and can suddenly transform your life when you least expect it.

When God's grace falls on you out of the clear blue sky, it's unmistakable. Few things on earth have the same kind of disruptive effect. In a negative, tragic sense, man-made bombs have a similar unsettling impact, changing lives dramatically for the worse. But when God drops a Grace Bomb, He disrupts life to restore it; His bombs are not weapons of destruction, but weapons of construction.

When I preach, I use lots of props and visual aids. The first time I presented unexploded falling ordinances with hearts in them, they looked like this:

In a story from the Old Testament, these Grace Bombs lovingly rained down on Gideon in order to help him conquer his fears. This stick-figure masterpiece will come to life when we start the second part of the book.

The juxtaposition of the words *grace* and *bomb* struck me as a redemptive contrast: taking a concept that has brought darkness and pain to our world, like bombs, and repurposing it for good. This is also a business that God is in: taking what is meant for evil and using it for good. Most notably, the cross on which Jesus died was a despised tool of war and national conquest, and God used it to bring about the greatest good the world has ever seen.

As a Bible teacher, I long to see people live out deep, spiritual truths in practical, everyday ways. So I thought, *If God grace bombs people, maybe we who have received His grace should grace bomb people too!* I reckoned that in a world of photo bombs, bath bombs, truth bombs, and some people still hanging on to the phrase "You're the bomb," the time might be right to rally an army of Grace Bombers who would drop tangible tastes of surprising love to brighten a neighbor's day. Going beyond random kindness, Grace Bombing could help us point people to the source of kindness itself.

Initially, I thought about creating an interactive bulletin board—where people could exchange services or discover and share needs—but that seemed too limited and centralized. We needed something more lightweight and low maintenance, something that would interest adults and be simple enough for kids to understand. Through a collaborative brainstorming effort with the creative team at my church, we designed a simple Grace Bomb card that anyone could hand out and a website to explain further what it meant to be grace bombed. These became the training wheels of obedience to our calling to love our neighbors with no strings attached.

When we talked to our congregation about Grace Bombing, we described it as a surprising gift that is intended to brighten a neighbor's day. We loaded them up with Grace Bomb cards to accompany any gifts, kind words, or other investments in their neighbors that God would lead them to offer. By equipping them with these cards, we were providing them with a tangible reminder that their neighbors may need an infusion of hope. We were also giving them permission to break the ice and do something unexpectedly cool for their neighbors, without seeming like a complete weirdo.

Then these regular church people got their bomb on. They didn't require explicit instructions; all they needed was a tool and permission. That's how the movement was born—a movement of loving our neighbors motivated by grace, not with random acts of kindness, but with intentional acts of love prompted by the Holy Spirit.

Loaded All Night

Now back to the daddy-daughter date. When Scarlett took it upon herself to initiate Grace Bombing, it signaled her innocent desire to bring Jesus into her regular day. This was a proud dad moment, and of course I wanted to fan her passion into flame, so I reached back into my backpack and put three Grace Bomb cards in the pocket of my jeans. This is what I call being *Loaded*, which by this point had a totally different meaning than in my college years when I was not taking Jesus very seriously. So thanks to Scarlett, instead of napping at home, we were out and about, armed with the intention and ability to break the ice with neighbors and brighten their days.

After discussing Scarlett's first-grade workload and dreams of being an Olympic gymnast, we dropped our initial bomb by paying for the meals of the two elderly women behind us in line at McDonald's. This was an anonymous Grace Bomb, which is where many people start out in their Grace Bombing adventures—undercover. Scarlett's imagination stirred with how that gift must have felt for the two women. As we left, she asked me to drive through Starbucks to buy a cake pop for her Awana volunteer teacher. This required a little more boldness, since Scarlett would need to hand-deliver this unexpected gift in person. That's when Grace Bombing becomes more relational.

Later, while all the kids were busy memorizing Bible verses at Awana, my wife, Kristen, and I had a short window of time to head over to our favorite local BBQ joint, Chad's. (Parents of small kids, you're welcome to steal this life hack.) Chad's has that wholesome, small-town vibe, though in a medium-sized town, complete with a giant iron rooster standing tall over the parking lot and vintage rock-and-roll memorabilia covering the dining-room walls. It's the kind of place that you selfishly hope remains a secret, while simultaneously telling everyone you know about it. We sat outside on the patio, where the hanging garden lights highlight the sparkling glaze on your wings, and I filled Kristen in on the daddy-daughter date.

Our waitress, Terry, was frustrated because the couple before us had skipped out on paying their check—yes, the dreaded dine and dash! Having waited tables in college, Kristen and I both knew how horrible that felt. Terry said that having to pay their tab wasn't the worst part, but it was the feeling of being ghosted—like the couple didn't even recognize their effect on another human being. Seriously, what's up with ghosting these days?

After Terry went to grab our drinks, Kristen gave me that look. You know, the look that says, *Are you feeling what I am feeling?* I knew this twinkle in her eye was either because I was looking especially dapper under the stars or because she was being nudged to grace bomb Terry to make up for the unpaid tab. Well, before you start singing, "Can you feel the love tonight?" the twinkle was for Terry, not me—and I was feeling the same thing. Using the remaining card in my pocket, we paid extra to cover the ghosters' meals and jotted words of encouragement on the bill, so Terry could feel a small taste of the love of Jesus.

We left to pick up the kids, smiling because we'd been able to surprise our neighbor in love. We figured that was the end of the story. But that final Grace Bomb, motivated by the encouragement of a seven-year-old, went on to impact more souls, as it hit another divinely intended target whom we hadn't even met yet: Kristi.

Picking Up Wings

About a month later, I ran in to Chad's BBQ to pick up a takeout order. It was our usual, the Governor's Wings with a side of sweet-potato waffle fries. While standing in line, I met Chad for the first time—the owner and maker of the special sauce. He and his wife, Kristi, had heard about the Grace Bomb we had dropped on their employee, and he told me how appreciative they were of us covering the extra bill. Then he motioned across the room to his wife, who happened to be there.

Kristi, who also works in real estate, thanked me for the thoughtful gesture and said she really liked the idea of Grace Bombing. She asked if she could share the idea with her business network—to be used as a tool for others to have a deeper impact in their communities. Here I was, talking to a stranger who was excited about grace, which is not always an easy topic to jump into. So before leaving, I told her to go for it—to leverage the cards and storytelling website in spreading the cause of loving our neighbors with no strings attached. Again, I figured that was the end of the story.

But after another month or two, I received a text message from a friend and business owner in the neighborhood. He sent me a picture of a letter he had received from his professional network. The title of the letter: "Grace Bomb." In its contents, Kristi had shared about the night we had dropped the Grace Bomb on Terry and then went on to write this:

Since then, I ran into the minister and told him how much this story inspired me. I asked if I could borrow the idea, and his eyes lit up with excitement. The website on the Grace Bomb card has a link to print out a card and some ideas of other acts of grace that have been dropped. So, I printed out three cards for each of our team members and put them in an envelope with $100 and charged each of them with delivering three Grace Bombs.

What they did was extraordinary! They each picked their favorite and gave me permission to share them with you. Mistie and her son went to Walmart and asked if they could pay off the layaway amount for two toys for Christmas. The manager was all smiles and happy to help. Amber and her husband pre-paid an adoption fee at the SPCA for a special needs dog named Lilo to help make her more adoptable. Emily took gift cards for coffee to a police detective and his team to thank them for all they do. Natasha and her kids used hers to help

Gary who is experiencing homelessness and often hangs out by the CVS on Riva Road. Megan and her kids left a gift card in a basket at Giant with a note that explained that if they could use a little help with buying groceries, to please use the card. If they had enough, to please leave it for someone who was going through a rough patch. And Chad and I used mine to pre-pay for breakfast at someone's favorite spot in honor of all he does to give back to the military community. The entire wait staff know him and were looking forward to delivering it anonymously.

The best part of all of this was our team saying how this exercise changed the way they think. They are now more attentive to people's needs and looking for ways to show unexpected kindness … to share Grace. In case you would like to try this out too … enclosed please find your very own Grace Bomb card.

Your friend and Real Estate Guru, Kristi

That was a great text message. Two things I was learning: simplicity spreads, and most people need practical, everyday help to break out of their comfort zones to love their neighbors as themselves. The multiplication of what started out as just one intentional act of love had traveled like a shock wave out to Kristi, then to her staff, to those impacted by her staff, and on to her business network who heard about these stories and were gently encouraged to try it—all with the warm undercurrent of Jesus working out His own plans in people's lives. The story was spreading wider and wider, and it was only then that I began to see some of God's deeper plans.

Simplicity spreads, and most people
need practical, everyday help to break
out of their comfort zones to love
their neighbors as themselves.

Ending the Silence

Several months later, on Palm Sunday (the Sunday before Easter), I stood up to preach a sermon and, to my surprise, saw Kristi standing in the back. It was the first time I had seen her in church, and after the service ended, she made her way to the front of the chapel to inform me that she had found a new church home and was ending a twenty-year silence with God.

In the months leading up to the Grace Bomb at Chad's BBQ, a few friends who follow Jesus had been reaching out to Kristi. One had given her the book *The Shack*, which creatively speaks of God's presence in hard times. They had invited her to check out church again, but she had been reluctant. Those friends had been tilling the soil of her heart to receive what Kristi called the third sign that God was pursuing her—the Grace Bomb. This was the act of love that pushed her to turn around, start walking toward Jesus again, and find answers to questions she had been holding on to for a long time.

We didn't get into it that morning, but later, over coffee, she let me into her story. Twenty years before, at a Dunkin' Donuts in Maryland, a young man named Charlie died in a senseless act of gun violence. According to Kristi, Charlie was the life of the party, the friend who lifted up the rest. He was the center of a group of friends who came together through a church and were all nearing, or had completed, college graduation. Before Charlie's tragic death, Kristi was part of that group, interested and intrigued by church, walking toward Jesus along with her friends. But slowly and painfully, after that fateful night, the friends disbanded, the church activity subsided, and Kristi began to walk away from Jesus—struggling with why God would allow such a bad thing to happen to such a good person.

A couple of years later, Kristi got married—with new hope and fresh wind in her sails. Her parents, who had been married for fifty-plus years, set an example of a fun, lasting, and joyful marriage. And that was Kristi's expectation and plan until another unexpected turn of events. At age twenty-five, after only two years of marriage, the wind was knocked out of her sails again by an unforeseen divorce.

The pain plucked at the same damaged spiritual nerve that left Kristi asking God again, "Why are these things happening? Are You even there? Do You really care?" She struggled with these questions and did not discuss them with God—or anyone—for twenty years, until about the time that a little girl ran up to her dad's car wanting to have a date and "grace bomb somebody." It turns out that God had been preparing that day in advance while simultaneously preparing Kristi's heart to receive a fresh revelation of His grace.

After connecting back into a faith community and pressing into her most difficult questions, Kristi found, in her own words, "relief, release, and peace." She discovered a comfort in knowing that, even when bad things happen to good people, God is there, and He does care. When she was intrigued by the Grace Bomb and investigated church again, she also investigated the evidence surrounding the divinity of Jesus, and the intellectual integrity of the Christian faith. She shared this with me over coffee, and a few months later, she would share it with hundreds more when she publicly declared her faith through her baptism. Kristi resolved that Jesus is who He claimed to be and that, even in the darkest of days, we can hold on to hope, because we can hold on to Him.

Starfish

Kristi had asked if I would participate in baptizing her. (And if that term sounds weird, or churchy, the baptism I am talking about is water baptism that represents an outward profession of faith, demonstrating an inward spiritual change.) But before that sweet morning, she sent me a message over Facebook asking if Kristen and Scarlett could be there as well. Kristi knew how that date night had unfolded, and it was not lost on her that a seven-year-old girl had pushed the first domino that ultimately had redirected her heart to Jesus.

In the quiet minutes before the service began, in the front row of the auditorium where we meet for church on Sundays, Kristi approached and leaned over to Scarlett to say thank you for being so brave in wanting to grace bomb people that night. Then she handed

Scarlett a gift bag with tissue paper that held a turquoise-blue, framed parable of "The Starfish Story":

> One day, an old man was walking along a beach that was littered with thousands of starfish that had been washed ashore by the high tide. As he walked, he came upon a young girl who was eagerly throwing the starfish back into the ocean, one by one.
>
> Puzzled, the man looked at the girl and asked what she was doing. Without looking up from her task, the girl simply replied, "I'm saving these starfish, sir."
>
> The old man chuckled aloud. "Young lady, there are thousands of starfish and only one of you. What difference can you make?"
>
> The girl picked up a starfish, gently tossed it into the water, and turning to the man, said, "I made a difference to that one!"[1]

Scarlett read with an inquisitive grin on her face, and Kristi whispered to her that Scarlett was like the little girl and Kristi, the starfish. The picture frame had a Grace Bomb card tucked into it. Today that frame sits on Scarlett's dresser in her bedroom. The aftershocks of grace were still reverberating, showing me that, as much as Grace Bombing is for our neighbors, it is first for the follower of Jesus to experience the growth and joy of putting into practice what Jesus tells us to do, starting with loving people in our everyday walks of life.

Patio Assembly Line

If Kristi's story ended there, I would be thankful and declare victory for Team Jesus. But as it turns out, the movement is still rumbling along and touching more souls with sweet tastes of God's grace. While still drafting the manuscript of this book, I came across this picture from the patio at Chad's BBQ:

Under those cloth masks are big smiles from Kristi (left) and some friends who came together to help assemble a surprising gift for the employees of the two largest hospitals in our county at a time when those workers deeply needed it. Through her role with a local community service organization, Kristi was already helping to organize the delivery of meals to those hospitals on Easter weekend. She then decided to grace bomb them by also providing dessert and words of encouragement from people all over the county.

Kristi inspired an online space where people could express their gratitude and encouragement to frontline hospital workers. Before the Grace Bomb was dropped, hundreds of folks sent pictures, videos, and genuine notes, like this one:

With five kids, including one who had cancer, we have had more ER visits than we'd ever thought possible. One concussion, one febrile seizure, one broken elbow, one kidney infection, and the biggie—a life-saving, fast-acting cancer diagnosis ... doctors and nurses and staff at AAMC have literally saved us time and time again. We owe them so much. This Easter, we give thanks for you—medical front line! We are grateful for your courage and selflessness, putting others above yourselves time and time again. Going above and beyond to serve the community. Thank you from the bottom of our hearts!

Jen

Several years earlier, in the back corner of that same patio, under those same dangling lights, sat two tired parents getting a little break on a warm Wednesday night. That mundane occasion led to a small step of faith—with the help of a card in my pocket, left over from a child's desire to love her neighbors. Her simple and unassuming act of taking Jesus seriously had shock waves that pushed out wide and deep. Faith steps are like that. Stepping into the unknown, toward Jesus and for Him, we may be used by God in ways we never would have conceived or imagined. God loves to bring about blessing far beyond our reach from simple obedience.

The Movement Ahead

Kristi is my neighbor. And she is your neighbor. She is behind you at McDonald's. She is in front of you in the fifteen-items-or-less checkout line. She served you your meal. She cut you off in traffic. She is your hockey coach. She is your real-estate agent. And she is a real person who may be enduring a long silence with God—or perhaps has never met Him. The people we see every day have stories that run deep, but on the surface, we'd never know.

A Grace Bomb dropped at the right time allows you to put love on display in a practical way—and love is an enemy killer. Isn't that how God works? Is it not His kindness that leads people to repentance? While the movement unfolds, we may truly show the world a new way to interact with one another—and get people looking up.

The impact of Grace Bomb on others is important, but there is more. At its core, Grace Bomb is a movement of obedience. It helps the church put into practice what we've been told by Jesus—to love our neighbors, to experience the joy that follows that obedience, and to leave the outcome in His hands. Some of us just need a little help getting back on track, to warm a heart that has grown cold for others. For the rest of us, we may need to build a faith muscle we have never used: putting Jesus' words into practice.

You may not be setting out to change a life when you follow the prompting of God to love a neighbor with no strings attached. But He might. Maybe even to change your life. You might only see a random event, but God sees a divine appointment. You might only see an average person in the mirror, but God sees a grace-built person who has been made to grace bomb people. Today the church is sitting on a powder keg of untapped potential. Consider Grace Bomb your match.

Depth Charge

Heavenly Father:

- Open my eyes to the neighbors all around me in my everyday walk of life.
- Remind me of the simple ways I can surprisingly show them Your love.
- As You will, use my small faith steps and multiply them for Your kingdom.
- Ignite the loving potential of Your church in my community and all over the world.

Beyond #Kindness

*Leverage the element of surprise to point your
neighbor to the ultimate source of kindness.*

*Or do you show contempt for the riches of his kindness,
forbearance and patience, not realizing that God's
kindness is intended to lead you to repentance?*

Romans 2:4 (NIV)

River Monster

Growing up, I spent most summers off the grid, since my mom was
a school music teacher who didn't work that time of the year. We'd
spend all summer "down the country." It was the rhythm of our
lives—nine months on, with school and business between Glen
Burnie and Baltimore, and three months off, unwinding with the
family on the river. This routine kept me out of a lot of trouble,
because *the country* is in the middle of nowhere.

Like in most countrysides, nighttime was great for stargazing
and telling scary stories to your younger sisters and cousins. My
grandmother Grace started this trend with my older sister, Kelli,
and me when we were kids. We'd often drive down to the country
early in the season with our grandparents, and to pass the time on

the three-hour drive at night, she would straight up freak us out telling ghost stories on the way. Later, we found out that she would just retell the latest Stephen King novel she was reading. There is nothing creepier at eight years old than to hear *Children of the Corn* for the first time as you are driving through cornfields.

As I got older, I happily took up the mantle of freaking people out during the dark nights in Deltaville. One hot Fourth of July night, my sisters and cousins were sitting on the edge of a dock. The river at night is romantic and also provides creepy cover, so I decided to leverage the element of surprise for a good scare. My objective was to pull "the merman," where you suddenly pop out of the water and roar, scaring the unsuspecting children. And yes, I was doing this as a grown adult, in case you were wondering.

I accomplished my first objective of getting to the beach unde-tected. Then I had to face my own fears of getting in the saltwater and swimming under the dock. There were often sea nettles in the river. Not to be confused with relatively harmless jellyfish, a sea nettle has long, stinging tentacles—proof that there are such things as sin and evil in the world. But it was a risk I was willing to take. I went into stealth mode and swam under the dark water to just the right spot, ready to spring into action. I paused, breathed out a few attention-grabbing bubbles to get them to lean in, and with full force pressing down barefoot on the sandy riverbed, I sprang out with a *roar*!

It was an almost flawless merman. I'm pretty sure I nearly got someone to fall off the dock. The only problem was that, when I pushed off, I was unknowingly on top of a clump of sharp oysters that sliced open the soft arch of my left foot. Kristen cleaned the wound over the bathtub, and the next morning I limped through the Deltaville 5K, but overall my merman plan worked.

The plan worked in large part because of the element of surprise, which, it turns out, is not just a good strategy for the River Monster. Grace Bombers, looking to brighten someone's day out of the clear blue sky, can benefit from that tactic as well. Take Maria and Joy, who were among the very first to ever share their stories.

Sick and Tired

Loving a neighbor while leveraging the element of surprise is powerful. Grace Bombing is like the River Monster meets Christmas. It is making a loving investment in a neighbor without the cultural guardrails of expectation. Giving without the birthday, holiday, graduation, or even crisis is giving that presses beyond what is merited or anticipated and looks more like grace. A gift becomes more than a gift when you leverage this element of surprise.

Maria received a Grace Bomb with no cultural guardrails of giving, and that context changed the impact that gift had. Here are her own words:

I was at the airport waiting for my flight, sitting at the gate with a terrible cold, and suddenly a very nice guy gave me a bag with tissue paper, a small box with cinnamon, ginger and honey, ear plugs and an iced tea. He wished me to feel better! That was one of the best surprises I have ever had in my life!

Now it is not typical that anyone would be super excited about what happens at an airport; that is, unless your flight is early or you get bumped to first class. But Maria felt the love of a stranger, who not only noticed that she was ill, but also invested the time, effort, and expense to run to the gift shop and prepare an impromptu care package for her.

Can you hear Maria's enthusiasm as she describes this as "one of the best surprises I have ever had in my life"? Even if this gift had come from a close friend who knew she was sick in bed, the care package would have been much appreciated. But how much more striking that it came from a complete stranger in an airport at a time when she may have felt alone?

Here's another example. Joy was working her shift as a server in a restaurant, where it is normal and expected for customers to leave their servers tips. What is not expected, however, is when a customer drops a Grace Bomb of extravagant generosity. Here's how Joy described what she felt:

I was waiting tables for lunch for my fourth double in a row. I was having the worst week when a sweet couple and their son sat down for lunch. Super sweet and super kind. They left me more than a generous gift. They restored my faith in humanity. Words can't begin to describe what their act of kindness meant to me.

What takes me aback are these two phrases: "restored my faith in humanity" and "words can't begin to describe." Those are strong phrases, stemming from a surprising gift. If Joy's rich uncle had paid her a visit that day and left a big tip, I am sure she would have greatly appreciated it, but it might not have stirred her soul in the same way that those customers did. What's the difference? The element of surprise.

Breaking the cultural mold of giving is often surprising, pleasantly disruptive, and potent—for the giver and the receiver! At the same time, this lifestyle may require you to run to the beach in the dark, face your fears of getting stung in the face by sea nettles, and even risk slicing your foot open, leaving you limping for a while. Taking Jesus seriously is not risk-free, and it will cost you something. But if you're willing to get in the water with Him, it is always worth it, oysters or not.

The Missing Link

Surprise giving that goes beyond expected kindness is part of Grace Bombing, but there is more. A Grace Bomb intentionally implicates Jesus, and by doing so, It points others to the source of kindness itself, to the God who is love. And while kindness might be popular and trending in culture today, there is something missing when love is detached from its source.

While kindness might be popular in culture today, there is something missing when love is detached from its source, the God who is love.

At the end of each day, when our kids finally give up the fight and go to bed, after many rounds of escapes, requests, and wrestling matches, Kristen and I usually have an hour to chill out—or more accurately, veg out. Nowadays, we watch different shows on our iPhones on the same couch. But once upon a time, before our Wi-Fi was strong enough to handle multiple devices, we actually had to agree on what show to watch. For what seemed like a decade, it was either the sitcom *The Office* or *Shark Tank*, a show where entrepreneurs compete for investment dollars.

On *Shark Tank*, we began to see a growing trend, in which the younger entrepreneurs were building into their business models ways to give back to a cause or a community. We could call it from the time they stepped out onto the carpet—particularly the millennials were incorporating this altruistic paradigm on the front end of their marketing instead of through typical back-end corporate benevolence. Sometimes it helped them get a deal; other times it didn't.

Ever since the runaway success of TOMS Shoes, with the "get one give one" feature, giving back has become a more viable option in the business world, or at least a posture to emulate. If you pay attention, you might notice that institutions like paying it forward and random acts of kindness are gaining steam. From grassroots movements to celebrity talk shows to major corporations, #kindness (hashtag kindness) is trending. Even my bag of chips tells me to be kind.

A few winters back, a big coffee chain had a poster in its stores that read:

The holidays are here, and good is in the air. Hold
the door for someone, connect over coffee, say hi to

a stranger, give perfect gifts to the ones you love. And once good starts, it keeps growing from one person to the next—simple acts of kindness that touch the lives of many. Because good is contagious and giving is too. GIVE GOOD.

Of course, it is good to *give good*, and in many ways, it is a celebration of our humanity. As human beings created in the image of God with a moral compass, giving and receiving kindness is a longing and desire that refreshes our souls—it is a part of experiencing life the way God intended it to be.

I tend to believe the best in people and assume good intentions when big companies or celebrities promote kindness. I think for the most part that their hearts are in the right place and that they are adding value to the world by their pursuit to *give good*. To all those genuinely promoting the unconditional love of a neighbor through practically giving back, I say keep up the good work. And if the bottom line grows bigger, then that is a win-win, since God invented work as part of His good creation too.

But at the same time, these generic kindness movements commonly have a missing link. While kindness continues to trend, and good things are being accomplished, they fail in carrying out an even greater purpose: intentionally pointing people to the source of kindness. Generic kindness and do-gooding terminate on kindness and do-gooding, not God Himself. Just look. Kindness typically elevates kindness. This is shortsighted, because while kindness provides a temporary sip of water, only the *source* of kindness can offer the wellspring that satisfies a parched soul. Grace Bombing bridges the gap and fills in the missing link by unashamedly citing Jesus as the key motivator of the goodness that is given. While kindness movements can be culturally driven by marketing and positivity, this is a movement driven by obedience to Jesus and the power of the Holy Spirit. One relies on humanity, the other relies on God. One promotes the goodness of people, the other promotes the goodness of God. The endgames differ, and the endgame matters.

Now you might say, "Pat, hold up there, buddy. If you start putting Jesus' name on something, you are adding conditions or strings, and that's not really a free gift of kindness. You are weighing down kindness with religious baggage."

Adding a simple step in giving people information and pointing them to Jesus, along with a surprising gift, doesn't add strings or change the gift in any way. It does add the ability for someone intrigued or interested to investigate the source of kindness who continually provides grace.

Is there a better way to introduce the greatest blessing than through a blessing, to introduce the source of endless grace than through a touch of temporary grace? Isn't this God's way? From what I can tell, when the world wakes up every day to a beautiful sunrise, God is leading out with kindness.[1]

One Grace Bomber candidly shared her thoughts about the difference between generic kindness and Grace Bombing and what adding the missing link did for her:

I was out running errands and unprepared to drop a Grace Bomb. My children and I were just running in quickly to get a few things, when we saw someone in need of assistance. We would have helped regardless of the Grace Bomb concept, but what was awesome was that, because of Grace Bomb, we now had a way to introduce the love of Jesus in a natural way. Once the bomb was dropped, the recipient told us over and over again, "Why would you ever do this for me? I can't believe this! I don't deserve this! Why are you being so nice? Why are you doing this?" I can guarantee you, without the Grace Bomb, I would have just left without telling her truly why we were offering such a free undeserved gift, and she would have just thought we were kind. But we were able to say, "Have you heard of Grace Bomb? Look it up!" She looked puzzled, and we saw her instantly get on her phone—likely to search it—as we drove away. I'm so thankful for the opportunity to grow in my faith and have this tool to teach me in such a simple way how to love in action and in truth. I'm praying for this woman and praying that with each Grace Bomb dropped I'll only grow bolder and bolder to share the love of Jesus with the people He made and loves.

Anonymous

As this Grace Bomber points out, adding the missing link to our kindness is also a primer for spiritual growth. The little tool that helps leverage the element of surprise while pointing a neighbor to Jesus also provides a workout that you might not have seen coming.

Friday-Morning Yoga

In my mind, I'm twenty-seven, and I'd like to think that I could pass for looking that age. But gravity and dad bod are waging an epic battle against my workouts, trying to slowly turn me into a centaur.[2] I still play ice hockey, and at men's league at the Naval

Academy rink, one of the guys told me he thought I was twenty-five, ha! He might have been drinking, though, so there's that. And the day after playing hockey reminds me that I am not in my twenties anymore. Injuries are taking surprisingly longer to heal these days. Given the multidisciplinary sport that hockey is, you can imagine my surprise when I got taken to school in a most unexpected arena: Friday-morning yoga with Kristen.

Now I know that tons of youngsters are getting their warrior pose on, but this particular class has a median age of seventy and is mostly women. There is one other dude, and I think he is ninety. The backstory with me and yoga is that there is no backstory. I stretch before hockey, and that is all this body ever needed. I can't crisscross applesauce and figured you'd never find me doing that weird yoga stuff. But I like spending time with Kristen, and I take Fridays off, so there we were. And when I sized up the elderly competition, I figured, "I got this."

It only took about ten minutes into the first class for me to recognize my overinflated ego and that "I don't got this." The instructor was asking me to use muscle groups that were sorely underdeveloped and to stretch into poses that my tight hamstrings took one look at and laughed. I was trying to man up, keep up, and not be a total noob, while sweating and straining to not break wind out loud. All of these stretches and holds looked so very basic, so easy—but actually doing them was a whole different ball game.

It can be like that when it comes to Grace Bombing in simple and everyday ways. When you hear Jesus say, "Love your neighbor," it sounds like a basic stretch, a simple balance—but putting that into practice brings to light the many ways we have room to grow in exercising the core muscles of our faith.[3] For some of you, it might have been a while since you've worked out; for others, this might be your first real time exercising your faith beyond a Sunday. As you'll quickly see, Grace Bombing is a posture that pulls on lots of core muscles of spiritual discipline. In other words, simple obedience can lead to dynamic growth.

Spiritual Conditioning

Grace Bombing requires that we stretch ourselves in a number of ways, and when practiced regularly in everyday life, we stand to get a pretty decent spiritual workout. Let me diagram a few of them for you.

Being intentional to carry out Jesus' command to love our neighbors will require us to become more aware of the people around us and the needs they may have. It is easier than ever today to stay connected with technology while simultaneously staying distracted from the people we walk by every day. This stretch gets us looking around and taking note of the people all around us.

As we become more aware of our neighbors, our compassion for them can grow. And where there is greater compassion, there is a more acute need for prayer. Hitting our knees, literally or figuratively, flows naturally from the stretch of greater awareness of our neighbors. As Grace Bombers, we may naturally find ourselves talking to God more—asking for courage, opportunity, and effectiveness through our intentional acts of love. Or sometimes just the quick, "Help me, Jesus, not to get stung in the face by a sea nettle." An increasing prayer life usually coincides with taking steps of faith.

Knowing when God is stirring us to drop a Grace Bomb is related to another group of core muscles: discerning the prompting of the Holy Spirit. A primary role of the Holy Spirit in the past was to bring to the apostles' minds the words of Jesus and inspire them to write those words down in the Bible. Today, the Holy Spirit aids us in bringing those words to mind and into reality at the right times. As I'll explain a little later, believers are endowed with the person and power of the Holy Spirit. He is a real, living being that helps us put Jesus' command of loving our neighbors into action.

Grace Bombing involves giving of our time, treasure, or talent in a surprising manner. To grow as Grace Bombers, in quality or quantity, we also need to grow in extravagant generosity. Because it's such a fun and life-giving lifestyle, we will want to *grow* in this area. Jesus is not calling us to go into debt by Grace Bombing, but rather to plan on growing as joyful givers, mindful that God owns everything anyway, and we get to redirect His resources to the recipients of Grace Bombs for His glory. God is the owner, and we are the managers. This is a discipline that requires self-control and faith in God's ongoing provision.

VERBALIZING FAITH

When these exchanges occur in your everyday walks of life—in the places where everybody knows your name and they're always glad you came—you are naturally associating yourself with Jesus and inviting future conversations, without creating a forced or pressured expectation. This is especially true when your Grace Bombing grows from anonymous to more relational interactions. Talking about the real difference that Jesus makes with neighbors is not a common practice for the majority of church people, not for a lack of desire, but perhaps from a lack of practice and spiritual conditioning. The more we create loving and fun opportunities with the love of Jesus, the more we have to be ready to give Him the credit and see where those conversations lead.

The Grace Bomb Instruction Manual

Are you ready to go beyond kindness and start your spiritual workout? All around you today are people whom God has put in your path, the people in your everyday routines, to perhaps surprise with grace and brighten their days. These gifts will be as unique as the situation calls for, drawing from the resources God has provided. I will dig deeper into some of these ideas in the chapters ahead, but you know enough now to get your Grace Bomb on.

The steps of Grace Bombing are simple.

1. Load

Put a few Grace Bomb cards in your pocket or purse and consider yourself a loaded weapon ready to drop a taste of grace. This book came with some starter Grace Bomb cards. If you're reading a digital format or you need to replenish, get cards and ideas at gracebomb.org. Loading up on cards is a critical step, because you are deciding in advance that you will be on the lookout for your neighbor. You are preparing to be a blessing, ready when called upon.

Honestly, some days I decide in advance that I don't want to engage with people, so I don't Load—and I shut down all opportunities before I even see them. So the first faith step is making a decision to be ready. I personally have a different mind-set when I'm Loaded—I feel more like a missionary.

Practically, Grace Bomb cards work in at least four ways. They serve as

- a reminder that you have been grace bombed abundantly in Christ,
- a prompt to look for neighbors with divine appointments on their calendars,
- an icebreaker to help you to get out of your comfort zone, and

- a way for your neighbor to investigate your motivation and be pointed to Jesus.

Keep in mind that Grace Bomb cards are not gospel tracts (explanations about salvation through Jesus, with an invitation to trust Him), but they are a way for you to become a gospel tract. Cards that break the ice with neighbors, while strengthening your faith muscles, also work the same core that you'll need to flex in sharing truth when that time comes. They are not flyers for your church, but help you, the church, fly.

2. Listen

As you go about your normal day, and are mindful of your neighbors, be aware of the nudge, that prompting or stirring that God may lay on your heart. When I say Listen, I'm speaking to the prayerful awareness of God the Holy Spirit putting a burden to act on your mind and soul, not necessarily an audible voice that talks to you.

The primary way that God speaks is through His revealed word in the Bible, and one role of the Holy Spirit in our lives today is to illuminate those Scriptures. If you've ever had the experience of reading the Bible or listening to a sermon, and something stood out and seemed to be hitting home, I suspect that to be the work of the Holy Spirit in you. It is our job to learn the Bible, and it is His job to help us apply and bring it to life practically.

Because loving people and carrying out good works are so near to God's heart, isn't it just a matter of time before He spotlights certain people in certain situations for us to bless? Maybe you'll see a barista having an especially bad day, maybe your server will completely blow your order, maybe your neighbor's washer and dryer will go up, or you'll have a super-friendly cashier at McDonald's who was over-the-top nice—and in some soul-stirring way, you may sense that this is your person.

Later on, we'll see more examples of this, along with ways we can inadvertently stuff our ears and limit our ability to hear God's still, small voice. For now, seek to be open, expectant, and sensitive to the stirring. Some of us have already heard plenty, so now it's just time to do it.

3. Let 'er Go!

This is where the rubber meets the road, folks. When you see the opportunity, feel the burden, usually you have a small window of time to act. Lead with your gift, then lean on the card to aid your explanation. God is in the business of orchestrating divine appointments, so let's hit those windows.

That's it.

That is all you need to get rolling: Load. Listen. Let 'er Go!

Can you imagine an army of Grace Bombers blasting our world beyond kindness? Can you envision the day when church people are the force driving the cultural conversation of doing good? I can, because this is our birthright. Love is our war to wage on the unsuspecting world that needs to be rebuilt by grace.

To help prime the pump, here is a quick exercise for you. Prayerfully think about the people you bump into regularly where you shop, work, eat, live, and play. If Jesus brings a face or a family member to mind, jot them down here, even if you don't know their names:

Neighbors:

_____

_____

_____

_____

_____

Now brainstorm a few resources at your disposal, then note them below. Keep in mind that surprising investments in your neighbors can come from your time, energy, thoughtfulness, creativity, expertise, talent, words, hard labor, and financial blessings. You'll hear about more examples as you read on, but if you are in need of some ideas, scroll through and read some of the recent stories that have been shared from Grace Bombers and recipients that we post on Grace Bomb's social media accounts, all of which you can connect to through gracebomb.org. That is also where I personally invite you to share your story and spur others on to love and good works.

Grace Bombs:

_____

_____

_____

_____

_____

Now let these two lists sit with you and go live your life! Stay Loaded, keep Listening, and see what happens.

Depth Charge

Heavenly Father:

- Thank You for being who You are: the source of kindness and love itself.
- Help me to start surprising my neighbors with unexpected grace, with the resources You have given to me to manage as Your steward.
- Lead me to the right person at the right place at the right time today to light up with a small taste of Your grace.
- Push me out of my comfort zone, and help me to grow by taking steps of faith that I am not used to taking with my neighbors.

The Master Bomber

Get to know the most powerful and notorious Grace Bomber of all time.

Have this mind among yourselves, which is yours in Christ Jesus, who, though he was in the form of God, did not count equality with God a thing to be grasped, but emptied himself, by taking the form of a servant, being born in the likeness of men. And being found in human form, he humbled himself by becoming obedient to the point of death, even death on a cross.

Philippians 2:5–8

Jesus Loads

In the last chapter, we looked at three simple steps to Grace Bombing: Load, Listen, and Let 'er Go. In this chapter, we'll see how Jesus serves as an example for each step, starting with Loading to drop grace.

In It with Us

A few years back at Christmas, I took to the stage to preach wearing all white. This was a stretch, because I usually preach in black—not for a statement like Johnny Cash or to look like a priest in a robe, but because I sweat like a boxer, and black is the most forgiving color when you are in front of a lot of people trying to act like your armpits are not shower heads. There I was—in white jeans, white polo shirt, skinny black tie, and white shoes—in what I've been told was one of the most memorable times that I've preached. It was memorable, not because I looked like I stepped off a boy band tour bus, but because, by the end of the message, I had intentionally ruined my fancy getup.

For that sermon, my props included a few bags of concrete mix, a five-gallon bucket of water, and a storage bin large enough to sit in, which I had labeled "Creation." I explained that the bin represented our home and life here on earth. Then, I poured eighty pounds of concrete mix into the "Creation" container, producing an enormous cloud of dust. After that, I added water and churned it, resulting in a sloppy mess. Finally, before the dust had even settled, I got into the container filled with wet concrete and sat down.

I went on to explain that the concrete dust and slop represented our mess—the brokenness, drama, pain, and sweaty pits that come with life after the fall in Genesis 3. I didn't stay in the container very long, for fear of chemical burns, but I pointed out that concrete eventually hardens, creating a situation from which it is impossible to extricate yourself.

Now, back to my uncharacteristically white outfit—it was intended to represent the perfection and purity of Jesus. My goal was to visualize the reality that Jesus "got in it" with us. He was not afraid of our messiness and brokenness. Preaching at multiple services, I went through several outfits that day, but Jesus only needed to get in it with us once to carry out His great mission.

In practical terms, being Loaded as a Grace Bomber simply means carrying a card with you to give to someone, along with a timely and surprising gift, to point the person to the source of your kindness. But in a deeper way, being Loaded is being physically, emotionally, and spiritually prepared—being ready to drop grace.

Jesus had to prepare to walk in the good works that His Father intended for Him, and that preparation first required a human birth. Jesus needed a body to incarnationally show up in the neighborhood. Similarly, for us, to be prepared is to show up in the proximity of our neighbors, to see them and be among them.

On the very first Christmas, in the fullness of time (Gal. 4:4), the promises and prophecies of the Old Testament prophets came true. A son (Gen. 3:15), from a virgin mother (Isa. 7:14), would be born in Bethlehem (Mic. 5:2), and in the words of the prophet Isaiah, would be called Immanuel, which means "God with us" (Isa. 7:14; Matt. 1:23).

These Old Testament prophecies are indicators that Jesus existed long before He was conceived of the Holy Spirit and given birth by the Virgin Mary. The God of the Bible has always existed as one God in three distinct persons. On the first Christmas, God the Son, the author of the DNA code, wrapped Himself in DNA and prepared to grace bomb us, by putting on flesh and getting in it with us. His gift required a body that was intended to be a sacrifice.

This is how John's gospel begins:

> In the beginning was the Word, and the Word was
> with God, and the Word was God. He was in the
> beginning with God. (John 1:1–2)

And then John described the incarnation by saying:

> And the Word became flesh and dwelt among us,
> and we have seen his glory, glory as of the only Son
> from the Father, full of grace and truth. (v. 14)

Jesus, the eternal Word, got Loaded, prepared, by putting on a body—ready for the mission ahead and willing to get messy.

Loving your neighbors happens most naturally when you are around them. Take for instance the response from this dad, who said, "I couldn't believe people were so nice. I was traveling by myself with my daughter and had so much to carry. Luckily the baby slept through the trip. I was grace bombed by a couple who helped with the luggage all the way to the parking lot, making sure I got to my car safely. I was so grateful that I didn't know how to express my appreciation. But I am glad they were there—thank you guys so much. Promise to do the same."

To carry this family's burden, these "nice people" had to be there. They had to be traveling in the same airport, aware of their neighbor's need, and physically present to carry the luggage all the way out to the car—just as Jesus had to be in close proximity to physically carry humanity's burden to the cross.

Divine Empathy

Growing in Grace Bombing leads us to grow nearer to our neighbors, not only in physical proximity, but also in awareness of what they may be feeling. The incarnation of Jesus meant that He became like us both physically and emotionally. He was sympathetic to our human frailty and weaknesses. While He experienced this in daily living, He also intentionally prepared Himself for His public ministry by feeling three common temptations in the wilderness.

All of the gospels except John's record the account of Jesus' preparation for His public ministry in the wilderness. This was a time of isolation when, by the end of forty days, His hunger and depletion made Him especially vulnerable to temptation. It was a real time and place, where Jesus was faced with three explicit temptations like we might face. In other words, Jesus was Loaded with all the experiences and feelings of human temptation, making Him that much more present with us.

First, Jesus was tempted to cut God out of His life. It sounds crazy, right, that this would even be a thing, being divine and all? But there He was, like a sitting duck, when the devil tempted Him, saying, "If you are the Son of God, command this stone to become bread" (Luke 4:3). In that moment, God allowed His enemy to tempt His Son to doubt He could be trusted for the basic provisions of life. Satan suggested that Jesus take matters into His own hands—to supernaturally create food—rather than trusting His Father to provide. You can be sure that, if you have ever doubted that God would provide for you, Jesus has felt that too. If you have ever been tempted to believe that spiritual nourishment is less important than physical nourishment, Jesus gets that too.

Second, Jesus was tempted to sell God out. The devil showed Jesus an image of power—a snapshot of all the kingdoms of the world, all at once, that could be His for the taking, if He would only worship a false god, the devil himself (Luke 4:5–7). Now, you might think it would be unlikely for Jesus to cave in to this temptation, since it would require false worship. But plenty of seemingly good people today are willing to gain the world but lose their very souls. Think about how tempting that might be for a thirty-year-old guy today—to see all the kingdoms of the world, with the opportunity to rule them. How might you handle being offered money, houses, cars, fame, sex, power, authority, and a blank moral check to spend anywhere in the world, and everywhere in the world? If you have ever been offered something you really wanted but it would cost your integrity or a piece of your character, Jesus knows that feeling too.

Third, Jesus was tempted to call God out. In this final attempt to shove Jesus off the obedient path of dropping the ultimate Grace Bomb of the cross, the devil tempted Him to force the Father's hand by coercing angels into a rescue mission that would verify His divine identity (Luke 4:9–11). Basically, His enemy's challenge was for Him to jump off the roof and make His Father catch Him. This was a power grab that sought to undermine God's authority. It would have been like telling God, "My will be done, now." If you have ever wanted to put God to the test by forcing your will to be done, Jesus understands.

Jesus got in it with us and was tempted like us. He was asked to cut God out, sell God out, and call God out. This was preparation. This was Jesus being Loaded through His incarnation. But unlike any other human being who has ever lived under the sun, Jesus was able to resist all temptations, while still feeling all of them. As the author of Hebrews put it, "For we do not have a high priest who is unable to sympathize with our weaknesses, but one who in every respect has been tempted as we are, yet without sin" (4:15).

Growing in empathy, like Jesus, is a key way that we prepare to grace bomb. We need to be close to people both physically and emotionally. One of the early Grace Bomb stories I received was from a police officer who said:

When I came in to work I had a letter in my mailbox. Inside was a generous gift card and an incredibly encouraging note along with a Grace Bomb. The note was incredibly genuine and more than made my day. The evening previous I had been talking to my wife about how discouraging my work can be at times, so the timing was perfect. I hope whoever left the note and card reads this, thank you very much!

Now, I don't know exactly what that letter said, but I do know what made it impactful—empathy. Whoever wrote it was able to intuitively grasp the kind of emotional place that this guy and his wife had been struggling with the night before. It was encouraging because it was genuine, and it was genuine because the Bomber got in it with that officer.

Being Loaded is being prepared. It is the intentional act of showing up in the neighborhood and being aware. Jesus left heaven to do this and showed up in our neighborhood, and through experience, He became even more aware of all the ways life hits us. As we follow in the footsteps of our Master Bomber, we are called to grow in these ways for the sake of others.

Jesus Listens

Being prepared doesn't guarantee that we will grace bomb anyone. On the night before Jesus carried out His ultimate Grace Bomb, He showed us the importance of prayerful listening.

The Watch

During my adolescent years, our church in South Baltimore had a tradition of staying up into the night, in a dark, cold chapel off the main towering sanctuary. It was known as "the watch," and it occurred every year on Maundy Thursday, the day before Good Friday. Not many people signed up for the watch. It wasn't glamorous, just a person or two quietly reading and praying, trying not to fall asleep. The occasional police or ambulance siren buzzing by on South Charles Street helped with staying awake. I was my grandmother Grace's wingman for the watch—it became our thing. More often than not, it would be just the two of us until someone else showed up to carry the torch around midnight.

As a kid, I was excited just to stay up in the city past midnight. I never really understood what exactly we were doing there. I knew the mechanics, of course, but I missed the point. Before the watch started, the priest took the Communion elements of bread and wine and moved them from the main altar to the little side chapel. This was to symbolically represent when Jesus left the Upper Room after celebrating the Passover and went out to the Mount of Olives and into the Garden of Gethsemane to pray. Just as Jesus asked Peter, James, and John to stay awake and watch and pray with Him, we were supposed to mimic that in the chapel. It was like we were commemoratively keeping Jesus company before the trials of Good Friday.

But as a kid, I thought of Jesus as a superhero—right up there with Batman and Superman—and I never quite understood why Jesus wanted us to watch. After all, He seemed to know what was going to happen before it happened. He knew that Judas was going to betray Him (Matt. 26:25), that the disciples would scatter (v. 31), that He would be led to the cross (v. 12), and that three days later He would physically rise from the dead (John 2:19–21). The Grace Bomb of the cross was a solo mission, after all, so what was the deal with watching at Gethsemane?

Now, when I look into the gospel accounts, it is glaringly obvious why Jesus wanted company that night. Jesus was just as human as He was divine, and it is human to want to be around friends at the most important times of your life. Think about a bride and groom before their ceremony: they are surrounded by their friends, sharing in the joy preceding the momentous occasion to come. Jesus, on the other hand, was not preparing for a wedding, but for a funeral.

These were the last and lowest hours Jesus would have on earth before willingly walking to His death, and He wanted His boys there. Jesus told His friends, "My soul is very sorrowful, even to death; remain here, and watch with me" (Matt. 26:38). When Jesus told them to "watch with me," it was the same as saying, "Stay awake with me." In the Garden of Gethsemane, having left behind the teaching and foot washing in the Upper Room, a shift occurred in Jesus' spirit. He was troubled; He was feeling the coming agony of sacrificing His life.

This garden marked the final lap of the rescue mission that was promised in the first garden. The battle in Gethsemane repaired the battle in Eden. And although the cross of Jesus was a solo mission, it did not have to be. His friends could have stayed awake to offer Him a touch of sympathy, a small comfort in an otherwise dreadful occasion.

But instead, they slept. The inner circle of the disciples couldn't stay awake, and the opportunity to be with Jesus then was missed.

And it was in this context that Jesus gave them one last lesson before His walk to Calvary. It is a lesson that applies to all Grace Bombers too. It is a lesson that got lived and taught right there in the garden, as Jesus sought His Father and listened in prayer.

Filling the Gap

In the second part of this book, we'll be looking at the barriers that might need to be blasted in order to grace bomb people and walk in the good works that God has prepared in advance for us. In Gethsemane, Jesus taught a master class on blasting through such barriers with one sweeping idea. Let me show you.

When Jesus entered the garden to pray, He gave us an example of what to pray about. Matthew's gospel tells us that, after inviting His friends to watch with Him, Jesus went "a little farther [and] he fell on his face and prayed, saying, 'My Father, if it be possible, let this cup pass from me; nevertheless, not as I will, but as you will'" (Matt. 26:39). The cup Jesus mentioned is a metaphor for the suffering He would have to feel. In view was the agonizing pain of the cross He was called to endure—incurring the full and just wrath of God against sin and evil. It is one thing to deserve such a punishment; it's another to be completely innocent and take it anyway. It's one thing to know your mission; it's another thing to carry it out when your human instincts are screaming at you to stay alive.

Although Jesus knew this was His path to walk, He still made His cautious and careful request known to the Father about the possibility of a life-preserving alternative. I could be totally off base here, but Jesus knew Abraham's story of when he was asked to sacrifice Isaac. Perhaps this was Jesus double-checking that there was no ram caught in the thicket, making sure that this was indeed the only way to forgive sins. As a human being, Jesus could feel His desire of the flesh to stay alive. In this case it didn't hurt to ask about the plan of salvation for the world, because Jesus was committed to the will of the Father regardless of the answer.

Reflecting on this, the author of Hebrews said: "In the days of his flesh, Jesus offered up prayers and supplications, with loud cries and tears, to him who was able to save him from death, and he was heard because of his reverence" (5:7). Through His reverent prayer, Jesus was heard. The Father answered Jesus, not by altering His course, but by strengthening Him to finish the race.

Luke's gospel gives us a detail that Matthew left out after Jesus' prayer: "And there appeared to him an angel from heaven, strengthening him. And being in agony he prayed more earnestly; and his sweat became like great drops of blood falling down to the ground" (Luke 22:43–44). Jesus' prayer was answered, not by avoiding the cup, but by being strengthened to succeed in drinking it. While He didn't receive comfort from His friends, He was given supernatural help to give His life as a ransom for many. Matthew said that Jesus then continued to pray for God's will to be successfully carried out (Matt. 26:42–44). The plan of the cross was confirmed, and Jesus readied His soul for the long walk to Calvary.

This reverent prayer time in Gethsemane would instantly become a deep spiritual lesson for His disciples and for us. Jesus woke up His friends by saying, "Watch and pray that you may not enter into temptation. The spirit indeed is willing, but the flesh is weak" (Matt. 26:41). Jesus was saying that there is a gap between knowing and doing. That gap is problematic, because it is the space where we can fall into temptation and away from doing God's will. He told us why—because the flesh is weak! But the gap is also an opportunity to be strengthened by God.

The lesson played out right there in real time. Jesus knew His mission and hit the gap before doing it. He filled that gap with meaningful prayer by which God answered Him and strengthened Him. He turned to the Father to make Him successful in obedience. Contrast this with Peter, who also had the opportunity to watch and pray, but instead slept. When it came time to do the right thing, instead he cut a guy's ear off (Matt. 26:51–52), and within hours, he denied knowing Jesus even after he said he never would (Matt. 26:35, 69–75).

Here is how this lesson so aptly applies to our lives today. We can know the Golden Rule and understand we should love our neighbor, but putting that into practice is another thing. In moving from knowing the right thing to doing the right thing, we must cross over a gap of human weakness. This gap contains our fears, pride, apathy, busyness, and even our hard hearts. In this gap we may be tempted to muster up the strength from our own bootstraps, but we'll likely end up sleeping and missing one-of-a-kind opportunities. We grow as Grace Bombers when we watch and pray, by turning to God to empower us to carry out our mission. We Listen in prayer, not only for who to grace bomb or how to grace bomb, but to become strengthened and successful in obedience.

Jesus Lets 'er Go

The results of Jesus Listening to God and being strengthened in the gap were full obedience, a holy bravery, and an unflinching faith walk to "Let 'er Go" on Calvary. From Gethsemane to the cross, each step Jesus took was a willing step of surrender, forward progress driven by a deep love. A few insights from the Gospels paint the picture for us.

His Last Steps

Jesus' walk to the cross began after Judas came to the garden with "a great crowd with swords and clubs" (Matt. 26:47), marking the abrupt ending to the watch. Jesus was ready for battle; Peter was not. Jesus surrendered; Peter did not. The Scriptures were fulfilled, and Jesus' friends ran away (Matt. 26:56). It was the middle of the night on Thursday, and He was marched like a criminal to the high priest and other rulers who had been plotting this capture for some time now.

It was a mock trial, at best, with false testimony and deadly intentions. The leaders among the Jewish rulers wanted Jesus out of the picture because He was a threat to their religious system. Although they had probably read the promises and prophecies about the Messiah, they rejected Jesus with blind self-righteousness. They stumbled over Jesus not fitting the mold of their conception of the Savior. But even this rejection was predicted in the Old Testament: "The stone that the builders rejected has become the cornerstone. This is the LORD's doing; it is marvelous in our eyes" (Ps. 118:22–23; cf. Matt. 21:42).

In this first exchange, Jesus pulled no punches when asked if He was the Messiah. Caiaphas the high priest said, "I adjure you by the living God, tell us if you are the Christ, the Son of God" (Matt. 26:63). Jesus replied, "You have said so. But I tell you, from now on you will see the Son of Man seated at the right hand of Power and coming on the clouds of heaven" (Matt. 26:64). Based on the visceral reaction of Caiaphas tearing his clothes and crying "Blasphemy!" it was clearly understood that Jesus had laid crystal-clear claim to His identity as God's anointed Savior. But spiritual blindness is a tough nut to crack, and instead of worshipping Him, the crowd jumped Him, beat Him, and spit in His face. God was bullied. And this was just the start of the walk.

At daybreak on the original Good Friday, the band of rulers marched Jesus to the governing authority in the land—Pontius Pilate. Pilate was no dummy. He understood the dynamics at play. He had no real grounds to punish Jesus and knew this whole event was born out of jealousy and fear (Matt. 27:18, 23). Pilate tried to push the issue over to Herod the King, who oversaw matters in Galilee but happened to be in Jerusalem (Luke 23:6–7), and Pilate even sought to release Jesus (Matt. 27:21). But the pressure of a possible rioting crowd, who were whipped into a frenzy shouting "Crucify Him!" pushed Pilate to make a call that went against his conscience—execution.

With so much emotion and activity, you might think Jesus was just a pawn being tossed around in a political power play—a minor character becoming a casualty in the larger social, political, and religious milieu. But Jesus was actually in control the entire time. He was deciding to walk along to Herod, to stand before Pilate, and to take the hits from His kinsmen. Jesus made this clear when He responded to Pilate's interrogation with "You would have no authority over me at all unless it had been given you from above" (John 19:11). This walk had divine oversight and orchestration.

Jesus' steps were calculated and thoughtful, intentionally leading Him to bear His cross. After suffering a beating that alone could have killed Him, Jesus carried His timber beyond the city and up a hill known as Golgotha, because the hill resembled a skull.

There Jesus was, ready to take His final step of obedience. He left one last bloody footprint in the dust before lying down on His back to be nailed through His wrists and feet.

Can you see that footprint?

Envision it in your mind's eye; look closely.

Now, imagine just for a moment that when you gazed at that distinct outline, you saw your own footprint. A size-ten Nike swoosh, a size-eight diamond pattern, the outline of your sandal. How freaky would that be? In reality, though, that step, and each one that led to the cross from the night before, was ours to walk. Jesus was on a march to stand before a holy God to pay the just price for sin and evil, and He was doing that in our place, as our substitute, as our Savior. When a gin Jesus took those steps so that we wouldn't have to.

Then as He hung compassionately on that tree, as He labored in breathing, the righteous wrath of God was being satisfied. This lasted three hours until a darkness covered the land. Humankind's greatest problem was solved with God's kindness. When Jesus knew that the atonement was complete, He cried out "It is finished" (John 19:30), and then in His final intentional act of surrender, He gave up His spirit. Jesus died to save others from their bondage and debt to sin, a debt He Himself never racked up. The Grace Bomb of the cross was dropped. And that Grace Bomb changed everything. Its impact was verified when, just three days later, Jesus, who had been as dead as a doornail, showed up again, more alive than ever. He appeared to many eyewitnesses, who were then compelled to share what they had seen: Jesus was alive.

Weapon of Mass Construction

Have you ever thought about what life would be like without this central act of God in human history? Can you envision your life without getting grace bombed by Jesus, walking the path to the cross and carrying out the Father's mission of love? I'd probably be secretly searching for answers to life's greatest questions while trying to convince other people I'm doing just fine.

Can you envision your life if Jesus hadn't carried out the Father's mission of love? I'd probably be secretly searching for answers to life's greatest questions while trying to convince others I'm doing just fine.

I'd definitely be uncertain of who God really is. Lots of options are out there: monotheism, the thought that there is one God. Polytheism, that there are a bunch of gods. Or pantheism, that god is just kind of in everything. Or maybe the atheists are right, and the universe just sort of popped into its design randomly by sheer chance despite the mathematical improbabilities. There is no shortage of options for a religious worldview, but the cross, and the unfolding plan of the cross, reveals who God really is. It is in the cross that we see God the Father sending God the Son, empowered by God the Holy Spirit, to accomplish salvation. We see that there is indeed one God, who has existed from eternity past in three distinct persons.

Without the cross I'd be confused about what God is really like. We live in a world where bad things happen to good people. This can leave us wondering, *God, are You there? God, do You even care?* The cross resolves for us that God indeed cares—enough to get in it with us and take on our pain and suffering. When Jesus stretched His arms out on the cross, it was like God saying, "I love you this much." In love, He gave us the gift of the cross. But more than love, we also see His holy nature on display. Being perfectly just, God cannot allow sin and evil to go unpunished. God settles all accounts because He is holy, and the cross shows us His holy wrath against sin while simultaneously offering forgiveness.

Were there no cross, and all I had to go off of was my jaded moral compass, I'd be working hard to tip the scale of my good outweighing my bad. This is the philosophical underpinning of most world religions: a heavenly scale of good deeds versus bad ones. But the cross clarifies that getting on God's good side happens based on what He has done, not on what we do for Him. The apostle Paul summarized this when he said, "For by grace you have been saved through faith. And this is not your own doing; it is the gift of God, not a result of works, so that no one may boast" (Eph. 2:8–9). Our boast is in the grace of the cross, a weak thing made mighty.

In a more everyday way, without the cross, I'd be keeping up with the Joneses. During college, I had a courier job that took me past a car dealership that was selling a 1997 silver Porsche 911 Turbo. I used to stop in the middle of the night just to look at that car and imagine my life with it. That represented where I was finding my identity—in the things I could buy and in the admiration of my peers. But the cross speaks a true word into my life as to who I really am. The cross tells me that I am loved by God and have been given access to Him personally. I don't need to keep running the race with the Joneses when the cross tells me that I have the precious ability to immediately wrap my arms around true love, true peace, and true joy. And if I am not competing for those things with my neighbors, I'm so much better able to serve them.

In terms of my relationships without the cross, I'd likely be holding grudges, not forgiving, or even seeking revenge. It can be hard to give something you don't have. Knowing that I have been forgiven by a holy God, and that He holds no grudge against me, sets me free to bend that grace to others. Paul reminded us of that too: "Be kind to one another, tenderhearted, forgiving one another, as God in Christ forgave you" (Eph. 4:32).

And knowing of God's perfect justice through the cross, I also understand that God gets the final word and I don't need to get revenge. Peter, the same guy who turned to violence in Gethsemane, went on to say after the resurrection:

> For to this you have been called, because Christ also suffered for you, leaving you an example, so that you might follow in his steps. He committed no sin, neither was deceit found in his mouth. When he was reviled, he did not revile in return; when he suffered, he did not threaten, but continued entrusting himself to him who judges justly. (1 Pet. 2:21–23)

Without the cross, I'd be carrying around my own burdens. I'd be carrying around a death sentence because of my sin (Rom. 6:23). I'd be carrying anxiety about the future, guilt about past decisions, and shame about past struggles and current temptations. But in the cross, Jesus makes an offer for all who are weary and heavy burdened—an offer of rest, forgiveness, and new life, as a new creation, bought by His very life. This invitation is not to become part of a religion but rather to be in a relationship with the Creator. It is an offer to become a grace-built person—and sent into the world with new and faith-filled purpose, as we follow in the neighbor-loving steps of the Master Bomber.

Depth Charge

Heavenly Father:

- Thank You for Jesus.
- Thank You for His perfect life, sacrificial death, and glorious resurrection.
- Thank You that He got in it with us, that He gets us, and that He pulled off Your plan of dropping the ultimate Grace Bomb of salvation on the world.
- May You cause me to become more like Jesus with every step of faith that I take in His direction.

Grace-Built People

You have been spiritually assembled for heavenly purposes.

> *For we are his workmanship, created in Christ*
> *Jesus for good works, which God prepared*
> *beforehand, that we should walk in them.*
>
> Ephesians 2:10

Grace Built

We build things for a purpose. Any manufactured or produced item has an intention behind it. Its maker has in mind a use for it.

Take the Lamborghini—a modern supercar built for speed and perhaps status. Contrast this with the minivan, which is built for practical everyday transportation. Or take even the Ford F-150 Raptor, which seems intended to make the guy driving the minivan jealous, because while it is not as expensive as the Lambo, it is slightly out of reach for the minivan guy. Not many country songs mention driving a minivan, which is disappointing. I can haul as much, if not more, in the back of our family van than most trucks—including a dog who long outlasted his life expectancy. We don't just drive a minivan—we rock it. You could say that is its purpose.

We too are built with a purpose. On one hand, our ultimate purpose is to be in a right relationship with our Creator. On the other hand, when it comes to other people, it is multifaceted and dynamic—like a diamond reflecting heavenly light from many angles, beaming toward all the different relationships we have and the roles we play, even when we are unaware of our illuminating presence. But God does make one targeted purpose clear for all of us when it comes to our relationships with our neighbors.

The phrase *grace-built* is not a term you will find in the Bible, but you do see the idea take shape in the apostle Paul's letter to the Ephesian church. In the beginning of chapter 2, Paul described the spiritual reality of human souls that, in the words of Jesus, need to be "born again" (John 3:3). He explained the natural-born state of people as being spiritually dead and separated from God. But then, good news burst onto the scene, as God rescued those trapped in despair, the spiritually dead, making them alive in Christ. After this hopeful declaration, Paul emphasized that this salvation is not activated by our earning it, but by our receiving it as a gift (Eph. 2:8–9).

All of this sets the stage for this declaration: "For we are his workmanship, created in Christ Jesus for good works, which God prepared beforehand, that we should walk in them" (v. 10).

In other words, Paul said that followers of Jesus are like a manufactured product, crafted like a poem, perhaps even a masterpiece. *Workmanship* means "literally, 'a thing of his making'; 'handiwork.'"[1] The big idea is that we have been rebuilt spiritually, from the inside out. Here is another way to look at it:

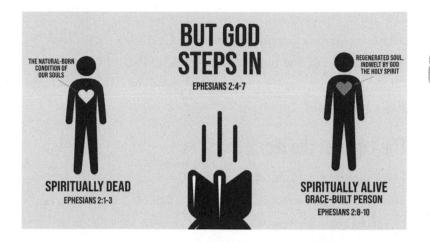

Now that we have rolled off the assembly line of grace, the question remains: What is our purpose as His handiwork? Is it for practical transportation? Blistering speed? To be adored by country singers everywhere? The answer is in the same verse: to do good works.

It turns out that being practically and intentionally kind, thoughtful, caring, compassionate, and loving, among other things, is the great intention of God for our rebuilt lives. In other words, grace-built people are meant to grace bomb people. All of your good works may not fall into the category of a surprising Grace Bomb; but every Grace Bomb is the good work of an intentional act of love, and every good work is an extension of the immeasurable grace by which we have been reconstructed and with which we have been supplied.

It's not only in Ephesians that God's Word spurs us on to exercising grace practically. In other places, the Bible tells us to "abound" in every good work (2 Cor. 9:8), to be "bearing fruit" in good works

(Col. 1:10), and to be "zealous" for good works (Titus 2:14). It reports that our good works are like "sacrifices" to God (Heb. 13:16), and they become a testimony to the onlooking world (1 Pet. 2:12).

Even Jesus Himself had some powerfully personal things to say about good works.

The Light of the World

Every morning, all around the planet, the sun rises, casting an illuminating net of warmth and reality for all of us. My mind is blown by the fact that photons blasted out of the sun about eight minutes ago flew through space at the speed of light and arrived here at this moment to allow me to see, and even to live. And that is just from our star—only one among billions of other stars, spread out over billions of other galaxies. The universe really is quite spectacular, and light itself is a wild thing.

When Jesus said, "I am the light of the world. Whoever follows me will not walk in darkness, but will have the light of life" (John 8:12), He made a bold claim, but not an entirely shocking one. It was bold, as He claimed to be the source of true life itself, but not shocking, because, well, He is Jesus, whose miraculous works continually confirmed His truthfulness. What is really shocking is that Jesus also called *us* the light of the world.

In His famous discourse, the Sermon on the Mount, Jesus said:

> You are the light of the world. A city set on a hill
> cannot be hidden. Nor do people light a lamp and
> put it under a basket, but on a stand, and it gives

light to all in the house. In the same way, let your
light shine before others, so that they may see your
good works and give glory to your Father who is in
heaven. (Matt. 5:14–16)

Children become familiar with this text as they learn the song
"This Little Light of Mine." Jesus called His followers "the light of
the world." As He rebuilds a soul that is alive to God, an eternal
flame is lit. His light blasts out through us, similar to the sun, bringing warmth and reality—not in theory, but practically, through
good works. Jesus defines the phrase "Let your light shine" as good
works that others practically see and feel. When you are intentionally loving someone, that person will know it, see it, and feel it.

Beyond enabling the mechanisms of life to function, light also
gives warmth. And warmth is an invitation to get closer. The Linnell
family are members at a community pool here in Maryland that
overlooks the narrowing end of the Severn River, a branch off the
Chesapeake Bay. Late in the season, this part of the river is usually
brown and muddy, and it's also warm. So when the kids have the
option to hop into the cold, crystal-clear pool or the warm, sketchy,
brown river water, they typically choose the river. That's where you'll
find them splashing around and spitting brown water out of their
mouths like fountains—because the warmth invited them in.

The love of Jesus is like this, minus the potential for flesh-eating
bacteria. It is the secure, comfortable place of unconditional love
that you just want to splash around in. So when your light shines, it
will feel really good to your neighbor. Grace feels good.

A Grace Bomb is like a small ray of a greater light that is free for the taking. A neighbor who felt one Grace Bomber's warmth shared this:

Imagine a single mother's surprise when she goes to pay on her son's presents in layaway and the thought of him not being able to open them until they were paid for two weeks after Christmas. Then I go in and find they were paid for! Now imagine the tears and heart-warming devotion I have for whoever made our Christmas truly magical. If I could only hug the person whose kindness touched our lives.

Every day, light hugs us—and this single mom wanted to hug light back. But ultimately, her hug is searching past the gift, stretching beyond the human giver, reaching unknowingly for the greater Giver. The warmth we give is the leading edge of the reality we know, that there is a greater Giver whose glory is the endgame of our kindness.

The Endgame

Without light, reality would be very hard to figure out. It would be an experience of continuously searching around in the dark. Thankfully, light shows us what is really there. The good works we are called to practice with and for our neighbors create opportunities to point them to spiritual realities of life with Jesus, who is the Light of the World. Don't miss the greatest possible outcome when our neighbors feel the warmth of our good works: the glory of God. The endgame of Grace Bombing is ultimately bringing glory to God through the thankful hearts touched by His grace.

According to Jesus, those who see Grace Bombs from a distance, or receive them personally, should end up giving "glory to your Father who is in heaven." The thanksgiving, praise, attention, and glory should not terminate on the gift itself, the human giver, or the concept of altruism, but on God, who is the motivation for giving, the source of the light shining through us, and the provider of every good and perfect gift.

Hold that thought. Right smack in the middle of writing this very chapter, an email popped up on my screen. It was from a woman named Amy, who I've never met but who had just been grace bombed.

I was in Sam's Club this morning to get a new tire to replace the one that a gnarly curb jumped out of nowhere and destroyed. I was standing at the counter debating whether to get one tire or two. The clerk mentioned that I really needed four tires due to their wear; however, I settled on two tires after a very quiet minute at the desk, debating in my head about safety, cost, and necessity. I paid and sat down to wait. Five minutes later, the clerk asked again for my Sam's card, and I thought nothing of it. When she brought my card back, she said that the gentleman in line behind me paid for another two tires so I would get a full set. SAY WHAT? I WAS GRACE BOMBED IN A MASSIVE WAY!

I wept; through tears, I prayed for the overly generous stranger and gave glory to God for His tender mercies. Needless to say, the challenges in my life are huge right now, as they are apt to be, but the impact of that moment was incredible and massive. So is God's steadfast love. The impact of this Grace Bomb and the perspective it brings will continue every time I see, sit in, or drive my car with its new shoes. Then, the follow on was that the clerk and I had a conversation about blessings, so I was hopefully able to pass some grace along.

Finally, this is what I shared with friends today on Facebook: Do something unexpectedly kind for someone today—a Grace Bomb for someone you don't know, even better. The impact on the person may be inexplicable, the example for others meaningful, and the blessing for you will be a treasure in heaven. All glory to God.

This was a fun and articulate little story, but even more, I was struck by how the recipient's attention was drawn beyond the gift and giver, to the ultimate source behind that small ray of light.

If the glory of God lies behind the good things we do, springing from the source of what's been done for us, then it makes sense that God is also somehow involved in orchestrating our good works, since He rightfully is honored because of them. When someone drops a Grace Bomb on a complete stranger, like Amy in Sam's Club, we might think that these are completely random acts of kindness—but with Jesus, nothing is random.

Not-So-Random

When people think of acts of kindness as random, it is usually because the kindness came from a stranger or random people. But Jesus clearly commanded us to love our neighbors,[2] which will include many random people—making the act not at all random, but instead a simple obedience to the expressed will of God. In other words, Grace Bombs are not random acts of kindness, but intentional acts of love. We are just doing what Jesus told us to do.

Grace Bombs are not random acts of kindness, but intentional acts of love.

Also, look back to Ephesians 2:10, where Paul provided this insight: "For we are his workmanship, created in Christ Jesus for good works, *which God prepared beforehand*, that we should walk in them." You could argue that Paul was alluding to God orchestrating the times and places of opportunity—the author of time, who lives beyond time, aligning the windows of time, for us to act at just the right time. You could go as far as to say that Grace Bombs are divine appointments that have been put on the calendar long ago, with purposes that we don't always see on the surface.

I experienced one such divine appointment, fifty-plus years in the making, a few years back when my grandfather's health began to decline. Those summers growing up "down the country" involved a lot of time on Pop's hip. My best childhood memories took place there, like riding my first motorcycle, falling off a roof, painting the hulls of boats that were precariously perched on top of cinder blocks, emptying septic tanks by hand, getting partially struck by lightning, practicing layups, and learning how to respect power tools, among other things that most ten-year-old boys dream of. I even have the name of my construction company picked out, if I ever start one, thanks to my on-the-job training: Close Enough Construction.

In Pop's later years, as my work and family life got busier, I became disconnected from his worsening physical condition. While his mind stayed sharp, his body began to fail him. Then one day I got a call to help with a little construction project at his house. The rod in his bedroom closet had broken off the wall, leaving a pile of hung clothes on the floor. This visit stood out, because it alerted me to how frail Pop had become since I had seen him last. It took the "random" emergency of the closet breaking to get me there. That day felt like a Grace Bomb to me in the gift of time I got to spend with Pop, as there were not many more times like that one before he died suddenly from a brain aneurism.

I believe God orchestrated that day. It was His plan for the piece of wood that held the rod in place on either end for over fifty years to finally give out. Upon my investigation, I saw that the rod had been positioned directly on top of a dark knot in the wood. The pressure from the weight of the rod bearing down on that spot in the wood was the culprit, as knots tend to weaken wood's structural integrity.

If my divine-appointment hypothesis is true, that means at some point God designated a tree, probably somewhere along the Eastern Seaboard of the US, to grow with a branch of a particular diameter that would form a two-inch knot, whereby after being harvested, milled, shipped, cut, and nailed into a closet in Glen Burnie, Maryland, would have the ability to withstand pressure more than fifty years until the grandson of that closet's owner would be blessed to see him on that particular day. Did God appoint a special tree to grow before I was born in order to bless me one day in the future? Well, that wouldn't have been the first time He's done that. I wonder what other "random" things He has planned for our lives in order to hug us with His light?

Look at what Jennifer said about Grace Bombing a mother and daughter whom she had never met before:

Going out the door at Sam's Club, there was a woman in front of me with a teenage daughter. She was so sweet and patient with this beautiful teenager that was mentally challenged. I gave her a card and some money and explained that the love I saw between the two of them made my day! She asked me if she could hug me and said, "Thank You, Jesus."

I was drawn to the woman's comment of "Thank You, Jesus." I thought that was interesting—that perhaps she was a woman of faith. We don't always get to hear the other side of the story for those being grace bombed. But a few days later, this mom, Jackie, found her way to the website and took a moment to share the following, showing me that this was no random incident, but a direct hookup from God through Jennifer:

I have a daughter who has cerebral palsy and severe mental illness! I was shopping at Sam's Club and had just completed my order. It was a stressful day. And I spent my last money on items, hoping to stretch out my food in the pantry. I had just finished praying! It seemed like I had just said Amen! WHEN I WAS GRACE BOMBED!

I'm convinced that God is able to bring about His desires in all kinds of ways that might seem random to us but have been calculated from eternity past for Him. There is nothing random about the plans of God. The neighbors around you every day are not there by chance. In fact, when Paul visited the Greek philosophers in Athens, he told them:

> From one man he [God] made all the nations, that they should inhabit the whole earth; and he marked out their appointed times in history and the boundaries of their lands. God did this so that they would seek him and perhaps reach out for him and find him, though he is not far from any one of us. (Acts 17:26–27 NIV)

God knows where every person is, and He can see all the potential ways that your light might impact them.

God is in the business of supernatural alignment to bring about the opportunity to carry out His will. I say "opportunity," because while divine sovereignty can lead you to the target, it's still our human responsibility to pull the trigger and act on those Spirit-led encounters. God lines up the windows of time, but we still need to jump through them when we sense the prompting to do so. Paul concluded Ephesians 2:10 with "for us to do" (NIV). God helps with that too.

The Nudge

Remember when the original Nintendo game console came out, and *Super Mario* was blowing minds? Right behind Mario was *Duck Hunt*, where you plugged in the gun—which tended to be glitchy—stood in front of the cathode-ray TV, waited for those little ducks to fly out of the bush, and then *boom*, you shot the ducks and watched them fall out of the sky. You might have even held the gun sideways for gangster-style points. That's how I rolled. These were the days before you were actually inside the video game. The key to *Duck Hunt* was to be ready, aware, and prepared to shoot. Before the ducks flew out, a rustling in the bushes alerted you to the coming opportunity. If you looked for the stirring, you were prepared when the ducks popped out. The bushes provided a nudge to get ready.

I believe God also gives us a nudge, a subtle stirring in the bushes of our spirits, that alerts us to the opportunities He has placed along the paths of our everyday lives. It's not a mystical process, but rather the prompting of the Holy Spirit that points us to Jesus and helps us to act on His commands, with loving our neighbors being a front-runner. You might call this listening to the still, small voice of God. You might call this a nudge. It might happen when something about a neighbor stands out to you, warms your heart, endears you in the moment, or alerts you to a great idea or an immediate way to put a smile on your neighbor's face.

Part of becoming a grace-built person is the removal of guilt and shame, being given the righteousness of Jesus, and becoming spiritually alive; but it is also being indwelt by God the Holy Spirit. I will talk about the Holy Spirit more a little later on, but for now, I just want to note that God Himself helps us get better at seeing, sensing, and feeling the opportunities: at work and on the way to work, at the gas station, grocery store, gym, school, yoga studio, or hockey game—among the people we see and rub shoulders with every day, who just might be feeling their way toward the light.

Olivia described the importance of discerning God's prompt-ings in her story:

I am still amazed how good God is and how He works! I was coming home from grocery shopping with my cold items in a little cloth cooler in the backseat and had every intention of going straight home. But God had other plans. I had only been in the car about a minute when God said, "Offer that woman walking alongside the road a ride." I pulled into the gas station just in time to intercept her. I called after her, but she kept walking. I pulled back out into the street with my hazards on and tried again. It wasn't until I got her attention and she accepted my offer that I realized she was deaf.

As rudimentary as my signing skills are, I told her I knew my ABCs. We found a way to communicate the entire time to her destination! The most moving part was when I pointed to my cross necklace and told her, "I listened." She was overwhelmed with thanks to Jesus and told me she had prayed for help! The excitement in that car was like nothing I had experienced! When I dropped her off, I gave her the Grace Bomb. I explained these cards are a good reminder of showing God's love to others and I told her how much she is loved. We hugged and parted with uplifted spirits. God is SO GOOD!

Olivia could have kept driving—most of us would have. I might have totally ignored that nudge in order to get home and dig into my ice cream, but she Listened. The result was an "excitement like noth-ing she had experienced." Having been prepared for this moment with her basic signing skills, she was able to communicate and con-nect. Those women arrived at not only a physical destination but also a spiritual one of mutual encouragement, where both were drawn closer to Jesus through a glorifying and completely unexpected car ride that God had in the works for some time.

I'm not saying that you are going to start hearing audible voices or that you are going to become Spider-Man, who can sense oncoming danger; but as grace-built people, we have been endowed with the indwelling Holy Spirit, who is able to illuminate God's truth in our hearts. And because we know for certain that God's will for us is to love people and He has prepared good works in advance for us, we should act when the opportunities fly out of the bushes.

It is a simple phrase—to love our neighbors—that is simultaneously one of the hardest things to actually do, even for those who were built for that purpose. Many barriers can keep us from walking in the good works God prepares for us. In the next section of the book, we will look at some common ones that I have struggled with, and with God's help, we will blast through them so we can grow to be a stronger force of light in our world. But before we turn to that page, have you seized any of your opportunities to grace bomb someone yet? Maybe now is a good time to see how those cards might work and have some fun surprising your neighbor in love.

Depth Charge

Heavenly Father:

- Thank You for making me spiritually alive to You and built for a purpose.
- Help me to carry out good works that You appoint and ordain for me.

- Allow me to get better at discerning Your specific promptings to surprise a neighbor in extravagant generosity.
- May You receive all the honor and glory as You allow me to warm my neighbor's day with Your light.

Part Two

Blasting Barriers

Ain't No Way!

Trust God's promises and watch them blast away your fears.

There is no fear in love, but perfect love casts out fear. For fear has to do with punishment, and whoever fears has not been perfected in love.

1 John 4:18

Hitting the Ramp

Welcome back. How did it go? That is, if it went. Grace abounds if you are starting this next section because you're currently laid back in a beach chair and just want to keep on trucking through the book and haven't given Grace Bombing a shot yet. I get it. If that is the case, remember to use sunblock and also that this chapter may prove to be helpful later on. I know from experience that when something looks cool or sounds fun but involves risk, it might not happen outside the walls of your mind. Fear can stop a cool idea from coming to life.

Case in point: I've always thought motocross and freestyle motocross (FMX) looked so fun on TV, especially as the sport progressed to even higher-flying tricks. As a guy who occasionally rides dirt bikes, I thought, *How hard could that be?* Around the time of writing this, I borrowed a dirt bike from a friend who happens to live down the street from a world-famous action-sports icon, who wrote the book on FMX and has miles of insane trails in his backyard—with hundreds of jumps, giant ramps that require airbags to land on, steep hills, and other formidable obstacles. It is amazing. When my buddy asked if I wanted to go there for a quick ride, he didn't have to ask twice.

When we arrived, my friend proceeded to take his hunting ATV over jumps and ramps, catching big air, while I proceeded to gently crawl up and down the giant hills, wisely avoiding the ramps and acting like a sane person. He asked if I had any interest in hitting one of the ramps. I politely replied, "Ain't no way." I was more than happy to keep my wheels on the ground. No surge of adrenaline or peer pressure was going to power me past the fear of ruining my beer league hockey career. I know myself well enough to understand that I don't have the skill and control necessary to safely land a 250-pound motorcycle after throttling it off a fifteen-foot ramp. It was cool enough just to see this backyard; I didn't need to become part of it.

Here's the deal: jumping a motorcycle looks cool and sounds cool in theory, but once you gaze at the ramp right in front you—and start to pee down your leg—it's a whole other situation. You have to push through some real fear and anxiety to hit that ramp. What if you don't land it? Twenty minutes into our ride, my friend hit a huge jump and then ran out of talent on the landing, which landed us at the ER to treat his newly broken collarbone. Fears validated.

Just like what I was feeling that day, Grace Bombing can be a scary proposition. No matter the size or cost of a Grace Bomb, putting yourself out there—exposing yourself to pain, hitting the ramp of representing the love of Jesus even in simple, nonthreatening ways—may come with a healthy side of "Ain't no way."

Crash Landing

I've experienced those fears in Grace Bombing, not unlike the self-protective impulse I had back on those ramps. A couple of months ago, while doing sermon preparation at a coffee shop, I sat across from a young girl who was having a loud phone conversation about some drama that was going on in her life. I wasn't eavesdropping as much as she was letting all the people in the crowded store know her life story. After the call, she remained in her seat for a while, and I got the nudge to grace bomb her.

I had Grace Bomb cards on me and was feeling led to pair one with a gift card, so her next few lattes would be free. I also wanted to tell her to hang in there. All I needed to do was hop up, walk ten feet, and Let 'er Go, at which time I simultaneously thought, *Ehh, I can do that later. I'm too busy reading about Jesus.*

So I put what should have been done in the moment on a to-do list. I literally made a note in my Moleskine journal to look for this girl later and grace bomb her. I left the store, and when I got halfway home, I felt so unsettled that I went back for a do-over, hoping she would still be there. But she was long gone.

Then I started to process internally, which Kristen tells me I have a habit of doing. *What was the reason for the fail? What was the worst thing that could have happened? She stands up and punches me in the face? Throws the gift card on the ground and stomps on it? Has an allergic reaction to kindness that sends her into cardiac arrest? Or maybe she just says, "No, thanks," and I feel rejected? Where did my nerve go?*

In reflecting on that missed opportunity, I think the fail was simply fear of possible rejection, which caused anxiety over taking one minute of my day to brighten someone else's. My failure to launch came from the fear of a crash landing.

One Grace Bomb story illustrates the fear of a crash landing coming true in someone else's life. Reading it is like watching someone launch into the sky, get squirrelly on their descent, and punch his ticket to the ER. To make matters worse, this real story came from a mother and young son. Nobody wants to see that crash.

In her own words, the mom, Helen, wrote in:

After church today, my son and I went to Wawa to grace bomb someone by buying their coffee with a $5 gift card, but particularly to have my son Jack do the Grace Bombing. He's 14. The first man Jack approached said an outright no to Jack and me, with an angry face and voice, in front of everyone in line. He then said, "I can pay for my own stuff." The cashier asked me what it was about. I briefly explained, and she said that what the man said was unkind and that what Jack was trying to do was good. I encouraged Jack not to be discouraged, so we decided to wait around and try again. In the waiting time, Jack asked me if I would do it, and he could watch and do it the next time. I walked up to a man in line who might have been standing with a woman and two little kids. We weren't sure if they were together. He also refused and said, "Give it to her," pointing to the woman behind him.

When I read that story, my first reaction was "Wow, this is not helping people start a movement of exercising grace." Then I got theological, wondering why, if God wanted Jack and his mom to drop a Grace Bomb, would this have been the outcome? I went on to feel mad at the guys for dissing my people. Finally, I felt responsible for setting Jack up for a fail.

All these thoughts and emotions rushed into my head, all in about a minute's time—my fear of being vulnerable had been validated! But if God builds people to bless people, then He has to have something to say about this natural fear of ours, right?

The Bible is particularly helpful in addressing our fears about hitting the ramps of taking Jesus seriously. In the Old Testament is a story about a guy named Gideon, who felt small and insignificant, fearful and anxious, when he was tasked to drop a major Grace Bomb. I want to walk through parts of his story with you to find how God melted his fears. Then we'll look at three loving promises we receive along with Gideon today.

Gideon in a Volkswagen

I first heard about Gideon when I was a freshman in high school, around the time when my sister Kelli started to get into the Bible. I came across a cassette tape of a sermon about Gideon that she must have picked up from one of her friends who had attended some big Christian festival. I listened to most of it in her car, a used, faded-brown VW Rabbit with a white tail. The white hatchback was a replacement for the stock brown one after a kid from the neighborhood shot out the back window with a BB gun.

Hearing this sermon was my first time being captivated by someone teaching the Bible. The speaker held my attention, and I was thoroughly caught up in Gideon's story. This was a shocker, since most of the preaching I had heard before could have rivaled

Ambien in its ability to put people to sleep. Seriously, I sat through many snoozers, pitying myself and the rest of the congregation, who quietly and respectfully were being bored to death during a sermon. It was as if the priest were trying to kill them, and only in that way would they meet Jesus.

In Gideon's day, the Israelites were led by folks known as judges. Don't think of the "Judge Judy, hearing cases" kind of judge. These judges were more like influencers and leaders in the protection or fortifying of the people against physical and spiritual threats. They were the nation's unifying leaders before Israel had kings like the other nations around them.

This was an era when God's people had reason to fear. They were oppressed and often plundered by formidable foes. These hard times were brought on by their own failures in fully obeying God. The season was one of an ongoing cycle of disobedience leading to distress, resulting in repentance and deliverance by God, who lovingly raised up judges to help and guide them. One of these judges was Gideon.

Gideon was an unsuspecting judge who was fearful of carrying out his calling. If you take some time to read about Gideon yourself, you will see how God lovingly provided reassurance and protection for Gideon that ultimately drove out his fears and left him in a place of utmost confidence that God would win an epic clash in which he was outnumbered 450 to 1—plus camels. Gideon learned that odds like those don't matter when God is fighting the battle.

Promises in a Winepress

We first meet Gideon in the Bible threshing wheat in a winepress. That was not normal—it would be like shucking corn in the shower.

Perhaps he was merely trying to stay quiet, but Gideon was carrying out his chores in hiding, for fear of his crop being taken by the Midianites, the bullies oppressing Israel. Just then the angel of the Lord sat down under a nearby tree and struck up a conversation with him (Judg. 6:11).

Keep in mind that Gideon was a self-described wimp who also thought his clan was the lamest in the tribe (v. 15). He basically admitted that he had been playing Dungeons & Dragons in the basement while his big, brawny brothers were out playing rugby. No offense to any of my fantasy gamer friends out there, but this was not the place to look for someone who had the brute force to battle Midian, which is why the angel's address, "The LORD is with you, O mighty man of valor," was completely shocking (v. 12).

This greeting took Gideon aback. His polite response—it appears that the angel looked like a regular guy—was just like ours might be, which was something like "Well, if the Lord is with us, why is all this happening to us? It's like God has just left us out to dry."

The angel didn't acknowledge Gideon's refreshingly honest response; instead, he revealed that Gideon was being tasked with dropping a huge Grace Bomb on all of Israel by saying, "Go in this might of yours and save Israel from the hand of Midian; do not I send you?" (v. 14).

It seems that the angel ignored Gideon's legitimate question about his suffering, perhaps because God had already explained, through a prophet, why this particular thing was happening—it was discipline, to correct their course. Maybe Gideon didn't get the memo, but it was clear that he was not ready to become the nation's military champion, even though the angel added this promise: "But I will be with you, and you shall strike the Midianites as one man" (v. 16).

What followed after the winepress scene was a series of unique signs for Gideon that God's promises would come true. A fire, a fleece, and a dream in the enemy camp were a few Grace Bombs from God that slowly reassured Gideon and lifted his fears so he was able to hit the throttle and jump the ramp. Flip back to chapter 1 for a classy stick-figure rendering of those.

Now I don't expect such things to supernaturally manifest in your life when you are hesitant to drop a Grace Bomb; those were specifically for Gideon. But the promises given to Gideon in the winepress do apply for every Grace Bomber who would come after him. These are promises to embrace and to remind your heart, when fear of getting out of your comfort zone or running out of talent on the landing causes you to freeze.

You Are Mighty

The first promise to embrace is found in the angel's greeting: "The LORD is with you, O mighty man of valor" (v. 12). This was quite the salutation for the seemingly insignificant Gideon. The angel spoke truth over him, calling him "mighty." Grace-built people are mighty, because we are instruments in God's hand.

This Grace Bomb fear hack is not finding strength in and of ourselves, but resting in the strength that God provides (1 Pet. 4:11). It is through our weaknesses that we become very powerful, as God empowers us to do those good works prepared in advance. A simple Grace Bomb dropped in love could be the very thing that turns someone's world right side up—not because we are superheroes, but because God wants it to. The hero in Gideon's story, after all, is God Himself.

The apostle Paul punctuated this point when he reminded the Corinthian church:

> For consider your calling, brothers: not many of you were wise according to worldly standards, not many were powerful, not many were of noble birth. But God chose what is foolish in the world to shame the wise; God chose what is weak in the world to shame the strong. God chose what is low and despised in the world, even things that are not, to bring to nothing things that are, so that no human being might boast in the presence of God. (1 Cor. 1:26–29)

Paul spoke these words to a church divided over personalities of various leaders. Like the world around them, they were gravitating to leaders who seemed more wise, eloquent, or powerful. He reminded them not to fall into that trap, and instead to stay unified, by affirming that God brings about His purposes through what the world perceives as weak or foolish, not wise and powerful. This is purposeful, so that in the end God receives honor and glory. God declares the weak things in the eyes of the world to be strong.

Just as the cross of Jesus, a stumbling block to the Jews and foolishness to the Greeks (1 Cor. 1:18, 23), was a mighty tool in the hand of God; just as Gideon, the weakling among his weak tribe, was made mighty; just as his three hundred men were an insignificant force made significant; so we, who are all Dungeons & Dragons players, are made mighty in the hand of the Lord.

God is able to do mighty things through us. He is able to take our faith steps and multiply them for generations. He has plans beyond what we could ever accomplish—and His great power is at work in you. So when you feel prompted to drop a Grace Bomb, and that nudge is met with fear, remind your heart that you are mighty, because you are in His hand.

When you feel prompted to drop a Grace Bomb, and that nudge is met with fear, remind your heart that you are mighty, because you are in His hand.

You Are Sent

The second promise that we share with Gideon comes in the form of the rhetorical question "Do not I send you?" (Judg. 6:14). Gideon was sent by the Creator of the universe, the inventor of life itself, the uncreated, eternal, spiritual Being who spoke matter into existence.

Grace-built people are also without a doubt "sent ones," from this same amazing Being. Jesus told His followers, "As the Father has sent me, even so I am sending you" (John 20:21). As God the Father sent Jesus the Son, so we are sent.

One implication of being a sent one is that we can trust that God will provide what we need for the jump and the landing. Another time, Paul said to the Corinthians, "And God is able to make all grace abound to you, so that having all sufficiency in all things at all times, you may abound in every good work" (2 Cor. 9:8).

As Jesus was given all things required for His mission, so we, the other sent ones, have access to this abounding provision. Gideon may not have thought three hundred men would be enough, but he learned that God gives us the grace we need, when we need it, in order to grace bomb others. This means that as we look to surprise our neighbors through giving our time, our treasure, or our talent, God promises to keep those accounts open and refilled. This is especially important when our fears in giving come from the worry of not having enough for ourselves. More than this provision, we have one final promise from the winepress: the presence of the Lord Himself.

You've Got Numbers

The angel told Gideon, "I will be with you" (Judg. 6:16). This speaks to our natural fear of feeling like we are jumping without a safety net—which may feel like the case when dropping a Grace Bomb. This might be our greatest promise to embrace in overcoming our fears. You are rolling with the King of Glory. If Jesus was literally sitting on the back of that dirt bike when I was encouraged to jump it, I probably would have gunned it.

When you and I step out to be a blessing, we step out with Jesus. Now, I get it, we can't see Jesus, touch Jesus, or share a meal with Jesus, like those first followers did after His resurrection. But Jesus made it very clear that, as we undertake His mission to make disciples, which begins with a Grace Bombing posture, He will be "with you always, to the end of the age" (Matt. 28:20).

That means when you go to hand someone a gift, pay for a meal, change a tire, share a kind note, offer a ride, give away a car, share your life story, or bring up Jesus to a friend, among other intentional acts of love, you are not alone. When things go right, Jesus is with you. When you crash and burn, Jesus is with you and is even able to bring about good from the pain of a crash landing. As we saw with Helen and Jack, not all jumps land without injury.

Assessing the Damage

What happens when a Grace Bomb doesn't seem to have a happy ending? What about Helen and her son Jack? They made two attempts to simply buy someone coffee only to have those cups thrown back in their faces. What's the deal with that?

If it's true that they share in the winepress promises of Gideon, then that means they are mighty, sent, and rolling with Jesus— though it doesn't necessarily mean they won't ever crash. But because of these promises, even in the crashes, we have hope, because God may choose to grow us through a trial, a broken collarbone, or even a rejection.

In Helen's case, she realized this after that day's events. She finished her and Jack's story at Wawa with these insights:

We tried to give a gift—a free gift—to two men who would not accept and were adamant bordering on rude. We wonder why this wasn't an easy thing to do with folks just saying, "Sure! Yeah, thanks." Why was this our experience? What did God want us to learn from this? For sure, we'll persevere. Jesus gives a free gift to all people, and so many say no, both back when Jesus walked the earth and now. It's the greatest gift of all. We got a tiny taste of that. How much more was our Lord Jesus rejected as He was said no to over and over. We are hoping that somehow God will work through our small acts of love.

Here, in the very rejection I was afraid of, God was able to bring a greater awareness of the person and work of Jesus into the lives of this mother and son. Taking Him seriously has that effect. The author of life itself desires to speak into our fears and draw us closer to perfect love, to Himself. That is the landing He wants for us when we step out in faith to put His love on display. While Grace Bombing is for our neighbor, remember it is also profoundly first for us—our landing is our jump. Our success is in the attempt, not the outcome.

I saw this expressed again through a wife's story that came in shortly after Jack's. She shared:

Grace Bombing people has been a blessing and a heartache at the same time. The heartache wasn't from a stranger or friend but from my husband. After being away for work for a week, I thought I would surprise him when I picked him up from the airport with his car completely cleaned! I spent two hours cleaning upholstery, dashboard, floormats and carpet, windows, tires, etc.! It never looked so clean or smelled so good. I was so excited to see his reaction. I decided to tape the Grace Bomb card to his passenger side so he would see it when he sat down. WOW. His reaction was disheartening and cut like a knife in my

heart. After a short hello, he immediately saw the card and exclaimed,
"What is this crap? I don't want this on my car—why is it here?" I
asked if he noticed how clean the car was and how good it smelled. He
didn't notice. His excuse was he had his sunglasses on, right? I was so
stunned and hurt by his response. Through tears, I explained to him
what a Grace Bomb was and how my church had started to grace people
by acts of kindness. After a very hurtful one-way conversation on how
I have changed and elevated Jesus in my life, I decided not to engage
in his rant but sat silently listening and praying. Twenty minutes after
arriving home, he apologized for his reaction and tone, and thanked me
for cleaning his car. I accepted his apology and explained to him why
helping others and showing others kindness is so very much needed in
this world. He is a police officer and sees the worst in humanity. I keep
him in prayer daily, for God to soften and open his heart. Even though
this experience cut me to the core, it will not hinder me from going
forward in grace bombing others and showing God's love!

In becoming ambassadors of grace in our love-starved world, we
will need to address our fears with God's grace and promises that are
true for us, as they were for Gideon. We'll need to remember that
success is in hitting the ramp and trusting Him to take care of the
landing, as He guides those who are mighty, sent, and walking with
Jesus. These promises will need to become deeply embedded, almost
like instincts that we can lean on as grace-built people, that help us
set sail from our comfort zones. To that end, a Grace Bomber named
Ron shared this:

I don't see myself as the kind of person who typically pulls himself out of his shell to do something outside my comfort zone. I was worried that someone might misunderstand my intent, or even worse, be insulted. And, it wasn't as if I went out looking for opportunities. What I have experienced in doing this [Grace Bombing] twice in the last week or so is that the opportunities are sometimes staring you right in the face, but you don't recognize it. What has worked for me is to just trust my instincts. In both instances, my bombs were accepted with a bit of disbelief and then sincere gratitude. In one case, I could see the entire demeanor of someone I have seen for months change from sour and menacing to a little smile and happiness. I really can't describe the feeling that came over me.

Dropping Grace Bombs is a faith step, and faith steps by nature have uncertain outcomes. This is freaky for people because not many of us thrive in uncertainty. To the contrary, we spend most of our lives trying to build a sense of security and stability. So faith steps seem ridiculous. But then again, so did taking three hundred men against one hundred thirty-five thousand. This contest turned out to be no contest, while sending Gideon on an adventure of a lifetime. Perhaps more sweet than the thrill of victory was the intimacy he experienced with God along the way. When all his fears were relieved, he worshipped. He drew close to God and not only walked into his purpose as a Grace Bomber, but also his ultimate purpose in walking with God. Would you want to miss out on that adventure? Ain't no way.

Depth Charge

Heavenly Father:

- Thank You that Your perfect love and promises are able to drive out my natural fears.
- When I feel the clear opportunity to grace bomb someone, but then resist, may it be Your power in me that causes me to hit the ramp of faith.
- I entrust the outcomes of my faith steps to You, Jesus. You got this, and You've got me!
- Remind me, Lord, that even now You are with me.

The Outsiders

Roll like Jesus when it comes to grace bombing people not "like us."

If you really fulfill the royal law stated in Scripture,
"Love your neighbor as yourself," you are doing
well. But if you show favoritism, you sin and
are convicted by the law as transgressors.

James 2:8–9 (BSB)

A White Guy Named Bob

I was thrilled when we test-drove Grace Bomb for the first time at another church in Glen Burnie, Maryland. Lighthouse Church was the first group of people to give Grace Bombing a try outside of my home church, and for me it was somewhat of a homecoming, as Glen Burnie folks are my people. The people of San Diego are my people as well, not because I ever lived there, but because I watched surfer movies as a kid and was drawn to the laid-back surfer vibe. I also got quickly swept up in the original *Beverly Hills 90210*, which further led me to believe I was Californian. What this looked like practically was a twelve-year-old landlocked kid with lots of hairspray riding a 2x4 propped up against a tree, pretending to surf. I guess I have different kinds of people.

It's interesting how we can quickly identify cultural markers that make us feel either included or excluded, like we are part of the tribe or not. One of the realities of living in a world that is fallen and under the curse of sin is that we also have a tendency to elevate our tribe over others—to deem different people groups or zip codes inferior.

As the Bible unfolds, we see that the problem of this hostility lies within the human heart, not because of any real superiority of personhood. In Genesis 1, we learn all human beings are created in the image of God, giving every individual person inherent dignity, value, and worth (vv. 26–27). But as history continues to play out, division and hostility between different races, religions, genders, political leanings, and worldviews still dominate headlines. Instead of celebrating our diversity as the human race as something that reflects the very nature of God, we consider our differences a curse. That's why the first story shared by a guy named Bob from Lighthouse is so profoundly simple and important.

I'll let Bob share in his own words:

My wife and I attended the 5 p.m. service today. I am an older, white guy and I ended up sitting next to a younger, black female who was by herself. About halfway through the service, I felt a nudge from the Holy Spirit to tell her that God asked me to tell her that He was so glad to see her here today and to remind her that He loves her. And to tell her that He has wonderful plans for her and that she needs to look past the ugliness of this world and focus on the beautiful things He has surrounded her with. And finally, He told me she could use a hug. She smiled and I gave her a big hug. I was hesitant to listen to the nudge, and I don't think I have ever done anything like this before, but boy did it feel good to listen and follow through. Praise Jesus for His love and inspiration.

Words of encouragement and a hug in the middle of a church gathering—the first Grace Bomb in Glen Burnie—cost no money, but it took Bob the "older, white guy" to get out of his comfort zone and Let 'er Go. I get the sense that Bob is not a big hugger, since he told us that he'd never done anything like that before. He was also in touch with some of the differences that cause division between so many today—in this case age, race, and gender.

Those are a few distinctives that can become springboards for superiority and then hostility, and the higher the degree of hostility, the harder it can be to love a neighbor on the other side of the fence, aisle, or tracks. And when hostility leads to aggression, say good night, as the cycle of vengeance can become all-consuming.

Jesus also lived at a time of extreme division. First-century Palestine was no stranger to political, socioeconomic, racial, gender, and religious division—all of which did not prevent the Master Bomber from dropping grace on those His tribe would have considered outsiders. In just one conversation, Jesus removed an entire barricade of hostility—one that might help us the next time we find ourselves in Bob's seat at the 5 p.m. service.

Bad Blood

The conversation I am referring to is in the first half of John chapter 4. It took place at Jacob's well between Jesus and a Samaritan. As was the case with Gideon, setting some time aside to read the whole story for yourself might be helpful, as I won't be addressing the entire account here. But for the magnitude of this conversation to sink in, it's helpful to have some of the backstory of the hate between Samaritans and Jews—a bitter rivalry of race and religion. In sports, most home teams have one rivalry that has been fueled by years of drama, whose true fans can hardly bear to mention the other team by name. It was like that, but without the ability to say, "Hey, it's just a game."

If you recall, in Gideon's day, Israel was a unified nation with no king. Later on, the nation divided, with separate monarchies in the north and south. The divided kingdom eventually fell, with Assyria conquering the northern kingdom of Israel, and later Babylon taking over the southern kingdom of Judah. To make a long story short, the Samaritans grew out of the Assyrian captivity in 727 BC—a new mixed people group of Jew and Gentile, who set up their own temple and worship practices and only held to a portion of the sacred Jewish Scriptures. The Jews rejected the Samaritans, as they could not prove their genealogy, and were considered ceremonially unclean and hijackers of the true worship of God.[1]

Fast-forward to Jesus' lifetime. The tension was thicker than ever. For the Jewish person, Samaritans were still unclean and to be avoided altogether. In fact, even the term *Samaritan* could be used as a slur. We see this later in John's gospel, when in heated debate with Jesus some Pharisees shouted out: "Are we not right in saying that you are a Samaritan and have a demon?" (John 8:48). It might have been the fact that Jesus' hometown was north, toward Samaria from Jerusalem, that made it a thoughtful assault on His character.

To make matters even worse, about twenty years before Jesus began to preach, some Samaritans had defiled the temple in Jerusalem by scattering human bones in the courtyard during Passover.[2] This was more than a playful stealing of a mascot before the homecoming game; this was a desecration of the most holy place of the Jews. And remember, Jesus was Jewish.

With these long-standing hostilities, Jesus addressed the conflict head-on and effectively removed the barriers that might have stopped typical rabbis from dropping a Grace Bomb on a Samaritan. He removed barriers that might have stopped this woman from taking a step of faith. He removed barriers that go beyond race—the same ones that might even be holding us up in extending grace to a neighbor.

The Fence

We could soften the animosity between the Jews and Samaritans by politely calling it ethnocentricity, or we can just use today's vernacular: racism. By the term *racism*, I am referring to discrimination that occurs based on one's cultural or ethnic heritage. Racism was one of a few cultural barriers that needed removing for the woman at the well. Let me illustrate it this way—imagine a fence, brought to you by Close Enough Construction, that contained these five barriers:

- Racism—this is the animosity and avoidance between the Jews and Samaritans I just described.
- Sexism—it would have been considered inappropriate for any man, especially a rabbi, to be speaking in public with a strange woman in Jesus' day.[3]
- Hot Mess—as we will see in the story, her private life was immoral and culturally unacceptable.
- Religion—her worship practices and her heritage were forbidden by the Jews.
- Misunderstanding—there were genuine gaps in her understanding of Jesus' true identity, which was a final barrier in receiving what He had to offer her.

For this unsuspecting woman, Jesus would need to remove all of these barriers for the delivery of His Grace Bomb. It was a Grace Bomb that sought to satisfy the very longing of her soul, one that would shock Jesus' friends, and it was a gift that shows us that no barriers should ever stand in the way of the kindness of the Lord, which leads people to repentance.

This was no random encounter either, as John told us that Jesus had to pass through Samaria—not because there wasn't another way around, but because He had a divine appointment with the woman at the well (John 4:4).

Four Little Words

At least ten times a day, my kids ask for a drink. It is a simple request, because they are thirsty or they need to bring their blood sugar up with a fruit juice. Sometimes I forget they asked and move on with another task—at which point they track me down like a heat-seeking missile to let me know that I forgot and they still need their fix. Pouring a drink, sharing a drink, chatting over a drink, and threading a pointy straw through a juice box are normal in families. But in Jesus' day, none of these were normal for a Jewish rabbi and a Samaritan woman in public in the middle of the day. In this abnormal exchange, it only took four little words for Jesus to remove three heavy barriers in the fence: "Give me a drink."

Here is the phrase in its context:

> And he had to pass through Samaria. So he came
> to a town of Samaria called Sychar, near the field
> that Jacob had given to his son Joseph. Jacob's well
> was there; so Jesus, wearied as he was from his
> journey, was sitting beside the well. It was about
> the sixth hour.

A woman from Samaria came to draw water.

Jesus said to her, "Give me a drink." (John 4:4–7)

Jesus was traveling through Samaria, and His disciples had left Him to go buy food from the town. It was in the heat of the day, and having traveled by foot, Jesus was hot, thirsty, and ready for a break. This wasn't a popular time of day to hang out at the well, as the women of the town typically came earlier or later, when it was cooler. Most likely, this Samaritan woman walked to the well at the time she did to avoid the other women, because of the shame or guilt she may have felt for having had five husbands and sleeping with her current boyfriend. In a small town, she surely had a reputation, and from a Jewish perspective, she was an outcast among outcasts.

Knowing all of this, Jesus flew in the face of sexism, racism, and shaming by asking a favor, striking up a conversation, and even proposing that He share her vessel for drinking. His contemporary rabbis wouldn't have been caught dead in this situation, but Jesus invited it. When you read about the people Jesus hung out with in the Gospels, this hat trick of surprising grace seems to be par for the course.

- Barrier 1, she was a she, but her gender was no barrier to engender hospitality.
- Barrier 2, she was Samaritan, an imminent threat to Judaism, but it didn't matter.

- Barrier 3, she was in an immoral relationship, but
  that did not cause Jesus to flinch in His pursuit
  of her.

There were many excuses to avoid this person, but Jesus ignored them all, as He saw a human being in desperate need of His kindness.

One picture to keep in mind from our era that captures a part of what Jesus was doing here is of the iconic moment when Fred Rogers (a white man) of *Mister Rogers' Neighborhood* shared a foot bath in a kiddie pool with the character Officer Clemmons (a black man) on the show. At a time when racial tensions were running high, and there was a lingering remnant of segregation mentality in certain places around the country, Mr. Rogers addressed it in his own way that even kids would understand.

In a similar fashion, beside Jacob's well, Jesus extended kindness in a way that was culturally unacceptable and then next-leveled it. In His "kiddie pool" was a person, not only of the "wrong" race, but also the "wrong" gender and lifestyle.

If that was how Jesus rolled, that is how we should roll too. For the follower of Jesus, there are no racial or cultural reasons to withhold grace from anyone, because everyone is created in the image of God and is one faith step away from the kingdom of God, becoming a spiritual brother or sister in Christ—a bond that runs deeper than blood. Indeed, the Samaritan woman needed to embrace the truth, but it was delivered to her on the bridge of grace.

And perhaps even more surprising than the way Jesus engaged this woman was why He did: to satisfy the deepest longings of her soul, a job she would find out that only Jesus can do.

For the Jesus follower, there are no racial or cultural reasons to withhold grace from anyone, because everyone is one faith step away from becoming a spiritual brother or sister in Christ—a bond that runs deeper than blood.

Melting Slurpees

On one July 11, Kristen wanted to drop a family Grace Bomb, one where we all got in the game. It was by far the hottest day of the year up to that point, and after leaving a playground with the kids, we noticed workers setting up tents for an upcoming event. We knew that on July 11, 7-Eleven gives out free small Slurpees. So I guess we kind of worked the system with this one by picking up free Slurpees to grace bomb the workers. Our goal was to deliver them cold and frozen, because how refreshing is a half-melted Slurpee on the hot-test day of the year? There is a reason they freeze these things. Ice cream? Have you ever left a bowl of ice cream half-eaten overnight only to be horrified by what you find the next day? Enough said.

I may have been driving a little too fast on the way back to the park, as the woman in front of us let me know with a one-fingered salute that had my kids inquiring about the odd hand gesture. I simply told them that, when you try to be a blessing, birds might start flying in to get you off your game. I had no further time to explain; we were on a mission, and the Slurpees were starting to melt. We sent the kids out to deliver what we hoped would still be a thirst-quenching surprise.

Because we have 7-Elevens, bottled water, and indoor plumbing, the significance of Jesus' next words to the Samaritan woman might get lost on most of us in first world countries. But in Jesus' day, and still for many developing parts of the world, a town could not exist without a well. Without water there can be no life. It can be easy to take the gift of drinkable water for granted, because we are able to freeze, color, and flavor our water, and give our free Slurpees away one day of the year.

The Samaritan woman's natural response to Jesus' request for a drink was one of confusion. She asked, "'How is it that you, a Jew, ask for a drink from me, a woman of Samaria?' (For Jews have no dealings with Samaritans)" (John 4:9). Then, Jesus revealed His point in engaging with her. It wasn't to meet His needs, but hers. He was there to offer her a satisfying drink, one that would quench her very parched soul. He understood that she had been drinking the melted Slurpees of the world, so to speak. And He replied, "If you knew the gift of God, and who it is that is saying to you, 'Give me a drink,' you would have asked him, and he would have given you living water" (v. 10).

By the well, Jesus introduced a new concept: living water. For the woman, this might have brought to mind a running stream, but Jesus was revealing spiritual truth to her. Just as actual water is a necessity for life, so living water is for spiritual life. The soul can't flourish without it. She didn't yet understand the spiritual metaphor, but she did recognize that Jesus was offering something better than what she had, somehow offering a lifetime supply of what she truly needed to live. Just who was this guy making such an audacious claim? What would He promise next, to open Chick-fil-A on Sundays? Which led her to call Him out: "Sir, you have nothing to draw water with, and the well is deep. Where do you get that living water? Are you greater than our father Jacob? He gave us the well and drank from it himself, as did his sons and his livestock" (vv. 11–12).

She was quick to point out that the well had been around and working since the Old Testament times of Jacob, the progenitor of the twelve tribes of Israel. Was Jesus somehow asserting that He was a better provider than the patriarchs? Jesus' answer was yes, because "everyone who drinks of this water will be thirsty again, but whoever drinks of the water that I will give him will never be thirsty again. The water that I will give him will become in him a spring of water welling up to eternal life" (vv. 13–14).

Jesus explained that the provisions of the patriarchs, her heritage, and the other "wells" she drew from were all falling short. Those wells didn't lead to the love she was made for. God wanted eternal life for her, and she could not attain that by following her Samaritan traditions or finding Mr. Right. Those Slurpees melt. Jesus' Slurpees don't. But for her to really experience this for herself—and for the Grace Bomb to land—her final two barriers needed to be removed. Jesus addressed her religion and His identity in the finale of their conversation.

Drop the Mic

Although she was still misunderstanding that Jesus wanted to impart to her the soul-quenching gift of eternal life, the woman at the well was intrigued by the prospect that she could somehow upgrade to indoor plumbing. She said, "Sir, give me this water, so that I will not be thirsty or have to come here to draw water" (John 4:15). Now, what happened next may seem like a weird shift in the conversation, but it was actually a move calculated by Jesus to open her spiritual eyes. He asked the woman to go and bring her husband back to the well. This was a setup. Jesus already knew she didn't have a husband, but instead she'd had five husbands and was currently with a man she was not married to.

While we don't get details other than these, we can safely assume that her private life was a hot mess—but as we've already established, that was no real barrier for engagement. So why did Jesus bring this up? Jesus was peeling back the curtain of His glory, revealing knowledge that could only come from divine revelation. He was beginning to show her who He really was. Jesus did not send the FBI into the village to dig up this woman's dirt; He already knew, because He is divine. This prompted her to say, "Sir, I perceive that you are a prophet. Our fathers worshiped on this mountain, but you

say that in Jerusalem is the place where people ought to worship"
(vv. 19–20).

One popular notion here is that, once Jesus started poking
around in this woman's sex life, she abruptly changed the subject.
"Oh, that guy. Hmm. Hey, how about those Washington Capitals?
Did you see Ovi get to 700 last night?" But I think something else
was happening. She knew Jesus was a Jew. She had just connected
Jesus with divine revelation. For her, a born-and-bred Samaritan,
this was hard to reconcile. While the two respective religions shared
a common origin story, they had a point of great division. It seems
that she was calling out the elephant in the room—her barrier of
religion, which obviously didn't stop Jesus from grace bombing her,
was preventing her from responding to His grace. Jesus swiftly and
decisively removed it.

In response to her inquiry about the proper worship of God, this
mountain or that mountain,

> Jesus said to her, "Woman, believe me, the hour
> is coming when neither on this mountain nor in
> Jerusalem will you worship the Father. You wor-
> ship what you do not know; we worship what we
> know, for salvation is from the Jews. But the hour is
> coming, and is now here, when the true worshipers
> will worship the Father in spirit and truth, for the
> Father is seeking such people to worship him. God
> is spirit, and those who worship him must worship
> in spirit and truth." (vv. 21–24)

Jesus did two profound things here. First, He declared Judaism as the winner over Samaritanism, by acknowledging that the Jews had received the full revelation of God through the Old Testament. The Samaritans self-selected to retain only a portion of the Scriptures, the first five books, known as the Pentateuch. Jesus basically said that the other prophets to come after Moses were legitimate and continued to communicate God's truth. Salvation was from the Jews, as these prophets would go on to reveal the promised Messiah, the bearer of salvation for the entire world.

But then came the mic drop. When Jesus described true worship, He leveled the playing field, telling her there was a new temple—a new correct place of worship. However, He said, it's not about finding a new location, but worshipping with a new heart. God wants worship from the human heart. He has always desired this kind of devotion.

Spirit and truth have two layers, the human side and the theological side. Plainly speaking, to worship God in spirit means to love Him from our spirit, our heart, that deepest place in our being, the seat and center of our emotion and will. Likewise, to worship in truth is to be honest and genuine, not hypocritical, such as praying one thing and intending to live another. The theological depth behind the phrase "in spirit and in truth" is that we are enabled to worship by the Holy Spirit through Jesus, who is the way, the truth, and the life. In other words, Jesus told this woman that the longings of her heart would be met as she came to know and worship God the Father, through God the Son, in the power of God the Holy Spirit.

Bringing It Home

So far, what this woman knew was that a Jewish rabbi, with some interesting connection to the true God, had broken the cultural rules of engagement and lifted barriers by asking a favor, only to turn around and offer her the deal of a lifetime. What seemed to be another guy who wanted to take from her turned out to be a guy who offered what she'd been searching for all along—true love and hope forever. This immediately called into question the obvious religious contention between their people, which He authoritatively addressed. This depth of knowledge, she reckoned, was territory only suitable to be clarified by the promised Messiah.

In the final two verses of their conversation, Jesus removed the last barrier for this woman: her misunderstanding of His true identity. The woman said to him, "I know that Messiah is coming (he who is called Christ). When he comes, he will tell us all things" (v. 25). Then, with no object lesson or metaphor, Jesus said, "I who speak to you am he" (v. 26). If any barrier of misunderstanding was still lingering, this blasted it away. Jesus was the Messiah she had been expecting to settle all matters of religious debate and, unsuspectingly, the person who could also usher her into true love, an eternal supply of soul satisfaction.

What happened next you'll have to go and read fully for yourself, because she seems to have right then embraced the gift of living water. And in her exuberance, she booked it back to the village to tell the people about the man at the well who very well might be the Christ. She immediately brought this good news home.

Jesus' disciples got back in time to see her bust a move. They were taken aback because Jesus was openly having a conversation with a

Samaritan woman in broad daylight. And then, to their amazement, they later saw an entire Samaritan village come to meet Jesus, and many believed, as Jesus and His disciples would stay another two days. So much for the Jews having no dealings with the Samaritans. Jesus was flipping the script and providing an all-access pass to the Father.

What this shows us is that God's grace doesn't operate within our fallen conditions. It is not withheld from any gender, race, religion, worldview, or current state of immorality. Lovingly, Jesus took away any barriers of this sort when He grace bombed the woman at the well and her entire village with the ultimate gift of eternal life.

If God's eternal Grace Bombs show no partiality, then the small and everyday Grace Bombs we are prompted to give shouldn't either. The Samaritans did not have it all right, but to address them, Jesus led with grace.

Tomorrow the headlines on Fox News and CNN may tell us that hate and division are more rampant than ever, and they might be right. But perhaps a growing army of Grace Bombers can help reshape the headlines, as more guys like Bob keep listening to the nudge and more sweaty workers, or women at the well, get a taste of Slurpees that never melt.

Undoubtedly, loving your neighbor can blast the barriers that our misguided hearts have constructed. Organizations, secular movements, legislation, and policy may all have some role to play in the pushing back on our hearts' desire to feel superior to people not like us, but only you, the church, can offer our world a new love, that creates a new heart, and a new compassion for all kinds of "outsiders."

Depth Charge

Heavenly Father:

- Thank You that You have created all human beings in Your image, and because of that, each of us has equal dignity, value, and worth.
- Search my heart, Lord, for where I am looking down on others or showing partiality, and give me the grace to own that and turn from it.
- I pray today, Lord, for cities and neighborhoods all over the world that are torn by considering others as "outsiders." May Your grace change and heal these relationships.
- Give me compassion and strength to give away Your grace with no prejudice.

Bad Samaritans

*Being a "Good Samaritan" all the time might be
impossible, but there is good news.*

> *For whoever keeps the whole law but fails in
> one point has become guilty of all of it.*
>
> James 2:10

A Popular Parable

With real Samaritans fresh in your mind, I want to look at the fictional Samaritan, whose story has become one of the most popular parables Jesus ever told. Today there are hospitals and laws named after this character, and you'd recognize his story as the parable of the Good Samaritan, based on a conversation Jesus had in Luke 10. Before I address why Jesus told the parable, let's recall the story itself. The tale contains what many hold as one of the most admirable ideals in the Bible—to follow in the footsteps of this man's extravagant generosity, which leads us to the revelation that our neighbors are anyone and everyone whom we encounter in our lives.

Jesus began the parable with a man, presumably a Jewish man, leaving Jerusalem for Jericho. The road to Jericho was a notorious route that left travelers exposed to the carjackers of their day. On the way, this traveler was jumped, beaten, robbed, and left for dead. The Jews hearing the parable for the first time were likely endeared to this poor guy who could have been their uncle, brother, or dad.

Thankfully, as the story goes, a priest, a man associated with God's work, came along. But instead of addressing the problem, he walked around the man lying in the road. We can speculate as to why: Was he avoiding becoming defiled by the blood? Was he too busy doing God's work? We're not told. Then, a ray of hope arrived in the parable when a Levite, another man who worked at a church, had a chance to redeem "Team God" and help this helpless man. But to no avail—he too made sure to avoid the crime scene altogether.

Enter the shocker in Jesus' story. A third man, a Samaritan, found the wounded man and did all the right things. He picked the man up, tended to his wounds with his own resources, took him to an inn, and left behind a blank check to ensure proper rest and healing. This stranger, a sworn enemy of the Jews, with the best of intentions, left an admirable demonstration of how to be a good neighbor, going well above and beyond the call of duty. This must have been a scandalous story to tell a crowd of Jews. But Jesus did, and He painted a picture of the high bar of loving your neighbor.

Now I don't know about you, but when I hear this parable, it makes me think, who in the world is this Samaritan? He sounds as if Mr. Rogers and Bill Gates had a baby that came out looking like Dwayne "the Rock" Johnson with a Grace Bomb tattoo on his neck—this guy was a superhero of neighboring.

Reflecting on this story, I can clearly recall three poignant times in my life when I completely missed taking up the mantle of the Good Samaritan. But in my failure to break the barriers of busyness, sacrifice, and apathy like Baby Rock Bomber did, I realized something deeper about the parable that I'd never seen before—that maybe I had missed the point of the story completely.

Purple "Love People"

In our first home as a married couple, Kristen and I were used to seeing grocery-delivery trucks, but not the ambulances. As newlyweds, we moved onto a quiet dead-end street in Severn, Maryland, her hometown.

It didn't take too long to meet some of the neighbors. In the small farmhouse to the left were friendly Mike and Kathy with their one daughter and their dog, Zeke, who could catch a golf ball in full nine-iron flight and only occasionally would swallow one. Then there were Norm and Marie in the Colonial across the street, another nice couple with two small kids. Norm and I bonded over motorcycles and cars, while Mike and I would chat about golf and the Bible. We seemed to be getting along pretty neighborly.

To help remind Kristen and me of what kind of neighbors we ought to be, I hung a makeshift sign above the inside of the front door of our house—a single sheet of paper taped to the wall that read "Love People" printed in purple, probably because I ran out of black ink.

Our neighbor next door on the right, in the rancher-style home, was more elusive and put our purple sign to the test. We had learned that she was a single, middle-aged woman who lived as a shut-in, due to her struggles with weight gain and inability to physically leave the house. We never saw her come out of the house but instead became accustomed to watching her weekly grocery deliveries roll in and roll out.

Perhaps it was meant to be, when me, a guy who worked at a church, and my wife, a practicing physician assistant in internal medicine, moved in next door to a woman who likely struggled with loneliness, depression, and severe physical limitations. This would be the kind of crack team that might be able to help, right? Here comes the priest and Levite to the rescue! Syke!

Over the course of probably three years, we made only one attempt to reach out to her. When we didn't feel any warm fuzzies after leaving a bouquet of daisies at her door, we went on with our own busy, newlywed lives, working in a church, working in a doctor's office, starting a family, watching the Peapod by Giant deliveries roll in and roll out. Eventually, the grocery trucks started being replaced by ambulances—until that final ambulance, in which she was taken to the hospital before dying of a preventable heart attack.

At that point, I realized we had permanently missed an opportunity to "Love People" that had stared us in the face every day for the first few years of our married lives. This opportunity was literally right next door in a white rancher with blue shutters. I can only describe what the house looked like, because I had never met this neighbor and still don't know her name.

What was the particular barrier that kept us from having a Grace Bombing spirit with this neighbor? If I had to put a label on it, it would be "busyness," I suppose. We were busy beginning a life together and starting a pastoral internship that kept both of us from applying our "Love People" sign to the neighbor we literally passed by every single day. The sign that was meant to encourage us was in reality the sign that condemned us. To this woman, we were the priest and the Levite. We were the bad Samaritans.

Fixer Upper

About a decade later, we came upon another rancher that afforded the opportunity to express extravagant generosity by way of a sacrificial gift, like the Good Samaritan, who was lavish in his giving to the stranger. Only this time, we were a year into regularly using the Grace Bomb tool and had become even more in touch with the promptings of the Holy Spirit. By this time, to not fully Listen and then Let 'er Go would be a real stinger.

Although Kristen was trained in the medical profession, she is more of a creative visionary at heart. In particular, she has a bent for knocking down walls and creating new living environments, in life and in real estate. Every couple of years, she finds a way to take on a new project. It might be painting, enclosing a deck to become a screened porch, or renovating a basement. But then, with the confidence inspired by watching many episodes of *Fixer Upper* and channeling her inner JoJo, Kristen found a dilapidated rancher that could have been bulldozed and forgotten. Instead, with help from the duct-tape skills of Close Enough Construction, she had the guts to take on a complete renovation. I'd like to say we had a more altruistic reason for the rehab, but honestly, we wanted to flip it fast for a profit. This was all about the Benjamins, baby.

We had never taken on anything like this before. It was a learning process, let me tell you. Everybody loves demo day, but that's just the start of a marathon. Before Kristen could get to any fun design elements, it took months to gut the house down to studs and address some major hidden problems with the foundation, basement, plumbing, electrical, wildlife, you name it—I lost sleep over it. At one point, I went man down with pneumonia in keeping this ball rolling.

After four months of working every night and weekend, with the help of many friends and subcontractors, and shedding blood, sweat, and tears while inhaling very questionable air, the house was finally ready to hit the market. On paper, we stood to come out with a decent chunk of change that would even serve as a way for Kristen to afford another project.

Along the way, while we were working on what turned out to be a gorgeous blue rancher, the thought crossed our minds and hearts to be grace bombing. Maybe it was the pizza-delivery guy who came to the house or the Home Depot workers who began to know me by name since one trip normally meant four more in the same day. We thought maybe there was something more to flipping a house in Glen Burnie and we should be on the lookout for a way to bless someone else.

But please, Lord, not this—anything but this.

The house had been listed high on the market, and we were getting lots of showings but no offers yet. I had taken the tool belt off and returned to life as usual, in church mode—waiting for a payday.

It was May 10, and as I regularly do, I was journaling a prayer before work. That morning, I was sitting outside a fancy juice place in West Annapolis, with a Bible open, when Kristen called in the middle of my prayer time. Since I was writing it down, I can tell you exactly what my prayer was:

Heavenly Father,

Thanks for this new day that you've made. As Kristen and I have been talking about the story we want to write with our lives, I surrender anything I am holding on to that would keep us from writing the story you want. Give me faith to trust what you say. Give me vision to—

The phone rang. Kristen had gotten a nudge, and I didn't want to hear it.

Later that afternoon, I had scheduled to meet a pastor in the area I had never met before. I had heard really encouraging things about his church and was excited to meet him. The blue rancher was only five minutes away from the new facility they were preparing to move into, so when I heard Kristen say, "This is going to sound crazy," I already knew where it was headed.

She wanted to grace bomb the house. She wanted to offer the house to a person we'd never met and take it off the market. I just died on the inside, but I also knew she was right. A Grace Bomb would mean breaking even and sacrificing the four-month investment of labor for the benefit of another family. For Kristen, the funds for her next possible project would instantly disappear.

To add a stamp of divine confirmation to this, four minutes into the conversation with Kristen, a stranger named Chris walked by my table, and while I was still on the phone, he politely interrupted to ask if I lived around there. He saw my Bible out and was compelled to stop and ask—and also to share his excitement about a church he had recently started to go to in Glen Burnie. Of course. "Funny you should bring that up," I told him. "I'm talking to my wife about that church as we speak."

Full-Isaac

Later that afternoon, the moment of truth came while sitting outside with the pastor. We had been talking shop for a while, and at the end of our conversation, it was time to talk about the house. Once I brought it up, I knew there would be no going back. But the next

right thing to do was to ask. Kristen had felt led to ask him personally if he was looking for a house. I had no clue about this man's
living situation. For all I knew, he was living happily in his forever
home. So I said something to the effect of "We just finished flipping
a house near your new building. Are you looking for a house? We'd
like to grace bomb you."

Have you ever had one of those times when you wanted to pull
the words back into your mouth?

As you probably have already guessed, the pastor and his wife
had been contemplating a move, and he was open to checking the
place out. Oh, darn. But real estate is tricky, and it wasn't like we
could just give the whole thing away, since we didn't own it outright.
Many factors needed to fall into place. First, would they even like
the house? Would it work for them? And second, what is the Grace
Bomb exactly? Just how much under the market value could we go?
This is where I personally wrestled and didn't fully sacrifice. This is
where I pulled a *half-Isaac*.

Full-Isaac is a phrase I use to explain when God tells us to do
something and He wants us to do it 100 percent. In other words,
He wants full obedience. When it comes to God, to obey is not a
scandalous or demeaning concept. Instead, it is a life-giving idea
rooted in the confidence that God's will is the best option for us.
Jesus even told us that His love language is obedience (John 14:15).

Back in Genesis 22, God called the first patriarch, Abraham,
to sacrifice his long-awaited son, Isaac, born to his wife, Sarah, in
their old age. Isaac was the first heir of many promised descendants.
It had taken so long for Isaac to come along, and now God tested

Abraham's faith and commitment to Him by having him walk Isaac up a mountain and take his life.

What a gut-wrenching step of faith this must have been for Abraham. Later, in the New Testament, we are told that Abraham figured that God would be able to bring Isaac back from death (Heb. 11:19). But even so, to surrender someone you love to a God who is invisible—and you're not sure why He's asking you to do it—is incredibly difficult. That's the nature of most faith steps. You have to trust that God knows what He is talking about.

Now if you're familiar with the story, you know God prevented Abraham from killing his son and instead provided a sacrifice by way of a ram caught in the bushes. But can you imagine the story if Abraham got to the altar and just put Isaac's leg on it? His left arm? Would that have counted as faith? God didn't ask for half of Isaac; He asked for the full-Isaac.

Our next faith step came down to dollars and cents. We were being asked to put the Benjamins on the altar, and I straight-up pulled a half-Isaac. In our calculations, although we'd be offering a price on the house that was coming in nicely discounted, it wasn't our absolute rock-bottom, break-even cost. At the heart of the thing, I was afraid of making that full sacrifice; I wrestled with that faith move. I was okay with being generous, but not with extravagant generosity like the Good Samaritan.

Hearing Clearly

Now when Abraham heard from God, it was very distinctly divine revelation to fully obey. This is true of the clearly expressed will of

God in all the Bible. But the Spirit-led inclinations to obey in certain situations—like when, how, and what to grace bomb a neighbor with—require wisdom and discernment. It's not like we turned to a page in the Bible that said, "'Your price is $225,000,' thus saith the Lord." But when God places a burden on your heart, you'll generally get enough detail to understand what He is asking of you.

Listen to how this worked out in Claire's life one afternoon:

I was picking my son up from school after a band lesson. I had baked cookies for a new neighbor moving in that I had planned on dropping off with an invite to our church for Easter Sunday. As I drove by their home, it looked like no one was home and might not be the best time to drop off freshly baked chocolate chip cookies and the invite. I drove on to pick up my son, and on our way back, I was sharing with him why we were going to take our neighbors the cookies I baked. As I was telling him and approaching our intersection to turn to go home, this woman was crossing the street with a look of extreme hurt which seemed to scream across her face. I felt so deeply inside that I was supposed to turn around and go back through the intersection and give her these cookies with a word from the Lord.

I turned around and my son said, "Mom, what are you doing?"

I told him that I felt deep down in my heart that these cookies were supposed to go to this woman. "If I can find her again, I'm going to give them to her."

He sat quietly and said, "OK."

I said, "We can make more for our neighbor, but these are supposed to be for her. I feel it so strongly."

I crossed the intersection, and there she was sitting in a bus stop booth alongside another woman. I pulled over and got out, with my heart in my throat, about to cry, knowing the Lord was pressing on my heart to obey Him. I got the cookies wrapped for the neighbor and handed them to her with a Grace Bomb card I frantically found in the bottom of my purse. As I handed them to her, I told her that these were meant for her, that they were cookies I had just baked, and I wanted her to have them. I told her that Jesus loves her so deeply, and that if she seeks Him with all her heart, she will find Him.

The woman sitting next to her said, "You are going to make me cry. You just said a mouthful."

I said, "I know. I'm holding back the tears myself."

She said, "God bless you."

I reiterated to the woman in need that Jesus loved her, and then left. As I was leaving, I prayed that the Lord would put it on the woman's heart sitting next to her to pray with her and that she would find Jesus today.

The prompting to drop a Grace Bomb can feel intense like this one did. When the burden is that clear, you know. You can feel it in your bones or, as Claire put it, your heart in your throat. And it was like that for me and Kristen with this sacrificial Grace Bomb on the table. After we gave the curious pastor our number, it was received with genuine gratitude, which then led them to explore the possibility of the house. They did like the house very much, but in the end, it was not going to work out for them.

Regardless of whether they bought the house or not, there was a problem. I knew that our first offering was half-Isaac, that I had fallen short of the picture Jesus painted in His parable. Kristen had put the offer in my court, since I was the one tracking the budget, and I failed to properly give this sacrificial gift. A lower offer may not have mattered in the big picture of the deal working out, but it mattered to God. It mattered to be fully surrendered, fully obeying, and fully listening to what we had clearly heard.

Pool Break

The third time I proved to be a bad Samaritan happened during one of the hottest weeks of the year in Maryland. The weather had just snapped back to a few cool, rainy days, and our kids were bouncing off the walls, needing to get some energy out. They were eleven, nine, eight, and four. So I figured to give Kristen an afternoon to unwind, I would take the kids to an indoor county pool. One little perk of this particular pool is the multiple lifeguards who help ensure the well-being of your kids while you relax in the adults-only hot tub. Hey, it takes a village.

A Subway restaurant is located not too far from the pool, and we had a little time to go inside and grab lunch before the swim session started. Only one other person was there ordering ahead of us, and I thought we'd be cruising to the checkout. But that guy had a mega-order, rattling off sandwich specifics a mile long from a list that could have been written on a parchment scroll with ink from a quill pen. For the time being, the kids were waiting patiently at a table. But I knew we were a ticking time bomb, and if one kid got restless, the dam would break, and the dining area would turn into a dance floor.

Our sandwich artist, Ramesh, seemed keenly aware of my dissonance and was working double time to get to us. He was the only person behind the counter at that time, kept a smile on his face, and stayed positive as he watched me glance back and forth between the kids and Shakespeare, who was still ordering. I greatly appreciated his effort to get to our order as fast as possible, which he eventually did, allowing us to enjoy our subs with enough time to catch the start of Dad's hot-tub time. While we were sitting there eating, I got an overwhelming urge that we should grace bomb Ramesh.

Although I didn't have a way to bless him practically in the moment, I looked out the front window, where across the street stood my credit union, which meant a no-fee ATM. I quickly envisioned blessing Ramesh directly with a $50 tip for his hard work. I thought this would be a nice surprise, since typically you don't tip folks in Subway. If anything, you might drop a dollar bill in the tip jar by the register. At the same time, though, I envisioned a quick drop and a fast getaway—because I really wanted to make it to that hot tub and didn't want to launch into a whole conversation about grace, or Jesus.

It had started to rain again when we left the restaurant and booked it to the ATM. My plan was for Ava, my oldest, to dart in, grace bomb Ramesh, and dart back while I had the getaway minivan running. But then, on our approach, things started to unravel. Pulling back into the Subway parking lot, we saw a hoard of people heading in for the lunch-hour rush; this would make getting to Ramesh behind the counter more difficult, but we had to try, so I told Ava to hurry.

I had barely parked when she jumped out into the rain, leaving the passenger door dangling open. Scarlett didn't want to be left out of the adventure and decided to join Ava in the dash. In her enthusiasm, she failed to see the door Ava left open and ran into it headfirst, promptly bursting into tears. As Ava looked back to see Scarlett now crying in the rain, her maternal instincts kicked in, and she ran back to console her, as the next ten people crushed into Subway. Meanwhile, Jackson, my nine-year-old, had been patiently waiting to break in his new purple umbrella, reasoning that now was as good a time as any to hop out and give his best rendition of "Singin' in the Rain."

One kid crying, one dancing, another consoling—thank goodness Max was young enough to have been locked into a car seat, as I was watching my fast getaway become a spectacle of wet kids providing entertainment to the onlookers in the dining room of Subway. Reaching Ramesh definitely just became more awkward. Ava and Scarlett finally ventured in to grace bomb him in between serving the new batch of customers. Then, we just needed to speed off into the horizon. But our getaway turned out to be as complicated as the drop, and it was then that God showed me the real mess of the day—my reluctant heart.

Messy Getaway

When the girls got back to the van, I was anxious to get rolling, as we had already created enough of a scene. Jack was still twirling his umbrella, caught up in the musical in his mind, and I was signaling to him, with an expression on my face that resembled a frustrated emoji, which said the train was pulling out of the station. Meanwhile, on the other side of the van, the sliding door was jammed open, and Scarlett could not get it shut. Both girls were tugging and pulling on the mechanical door that had all of a sudden frozen up. Max wasn't sure which direction to look—both were equally entertaining. I took a few deep breaths, as the seconds felt like minutes. If all you had to go on was my blood pressure in the moment, you would have thought we were literally robbing a bank. Who knew attempting to be the Good Samaritan would create such anxiety?

This scene caused a delay long enough for me to see Ramesh leaving his post and walking to the door, as his customers watched in bewilderment. I realized then that my cover was completely blown, and I may have just incited a small riot of hangry people inside. Ramesh only came as far as the restaurant door to offer a smile and a thumbs-up, but his boss—or perhaps wife, I'm not sure—who I was only now seeing for the first time, quickly followed behind him. She walked out into the parking lot, undeterred by the rain, to my now-rolled-down window to express her confusion in broken English: "Why would you do this? This is too much! Come back in the store and have whatever you want! This is too much!"

Cornered with no place to hide, a clarity then snapped in my mind and shot to my heart, as I explained that this was a gift, like the grace that we have been given from Jesus, a name that it seemed she had never considered before. I told her that Jesus, who we learn about in the Bible, loves people very much, and His love is a free gift. I thought, *Wow, I think she is hearing this for the first time.*

After that surprisingly meaningful exchange, which I had been fighting so hard to avoid, I learned that the real problem wasn't my hyper kids or the malfunctioning minivan, but my avoidance of what God wanted to happen. I wanted to get to a hot tub; God wanted to get to a heart. I wanted to stay comfortable in my little bubble; God wanted to use us to reach another nation right there in Subway. I wanted fast service and then a fast getaway; He wanted us to linger to explain the source of our kindness.

My reluctance, stemming from a selfish desire to hurry up and relax, was another reality check that being like the Good Samaritan sure is a lot harder than it looks. But maybe that is the point. Maybe the point of the parable of the Good Samaritan is that we don't live up to the standard of the Good Samaritan. But if that is the case, why tell the story at all?

Maybe the point of the parable of the Good Samaritan is that we don't live up to the standard of the Good Samaritan.

Heaven's Humility

The context of the parable unlocks the purpose of the parable. When you go back to look at the conversation Jesus was having that prompted the parable about the Good Samaritan, you can then discern the main point of the parable itself. And as it turns out, while determining who our neighbors are and what standard we should shoot for in loving them does not make for a bad life application—and can inspire some nice sermons—Jesus seems to have been communicating an altogether different message.

The gospel writer Luke told us:

> And behold, a lawyer stood up to put him to the test, saying, "Teacher, what shall I do to inherit eternal life?" He said to him, "What is written in the Law? How do you read it?" And he answered, "You shall love the Lord your God with all your heart and with all your soul and with all your strength and with all your mind, and your neighbor as yourself." And he said to him, "You have answered correctly; do this, and you will live." (Luke 10:25–28)

A lawyer, perhaps a Pharisee, who was intent on backing Jesus into a theological corner, first asked the question "What shall I do to inherit eternal life?" This was the primary question that Jesus' parable was meant to answer. But the lawyer apparently felt that he already knew the answers from Scripture—to love God and love people. Surprisingly, Jesus affirmed this. In fact, Jesus later highlighted these as the greatest of the commandments (Matt. 22:37–40). It was as though Jesus was saying, "Yes, here is the ticket to heaven: if you can check these boxes of loving God and loving people, then, Mr. Lawyer, you are good to go."

Then Luke gave us this little insight: "But he, desiring to justify himself, said to Jesus, 'And who is my neighbor?'" (Luke 10:29).

This is important. His motive, his heart's disposition, was one of self-justification. He initiated the debate over who our neighbors are, which Jesus did address, but now we see the heart condition that Jesus wanted to change.

This lawyer, who was self-justifying, or self-righteous, probably also assumed that he *was* able to check the boxes of loving God and loving people, thus punching his own ticket to heaven. This lawyer's greatest problem was not finding the proper definition of a neighbor but waking up to the reality that he couldn't love his neighbors as himself, at least not in the way God desires.

Enter the parable of the Good Samaritan. In effect, Jesus' challenge to the lawyer was something like this: "When was the last time you went out of your way to care for a neighbor? And not just any neighbor—how about a sworn enemy, the people who defiled the temple some years ago, the people who you'll go out of your way to avoid coming into contact with? When was the last time you left a blank check for that person? When was the last time you gave away four months of your time and profit to a stranger? Heck, when did you even delay something you were looking forward to, to be more present in the moment? That, friend, is the standard God requires, and it is a perfect standard—one that always gets it right, with everybody, always."

The Good Samaritan paints an aspirational picture indeed, but it was painted for a person who was convinced he was keeping the royal law of love, to show him that he too was falling short. And as the logic follows, anyone who falls short of God's commands is in desperate need of a Savior.

The main point of the parable of the Good Samaritan was to show the self-righteous lawyer that he could not punch his own ticket to heaven. Indeed, he needed a Savior. The answer to his question "What shall I do to inherit eternal life?" was standing right there before him. Jesus was revealing his greatest spiritual need—to have a poor spirit, not a self-righteous one. Thankfully, when we come to the realization that we can't punch our own tickets to heaven, Jesus comes to the rescue as our Good Samaritan.

So what does all this have to do with Grace Bombing? It comes down to humility, the flip side of self-righteousness. Humility involves having a "poor spirit" (Matt. 5:3) that recognizes that, without a hero, we are dead in the streets. But in rush the warm, flowing waters of grace, from a Rescuer who is not self-absorbed, stingy, or too busy, and who covers us and carries us away to safety, healing, and a new lease on life. Those waters have a weathering effect on a hard heart, making it softer, kinder, and more likely, in the words of Jesus to the lawyer, to "go and do likewise," when it comes to our neighbors in the ranchers and restaurants in our everyday lives.

Depth Charge

Heavenly Father:

- Thank You for sending Jesus, our Good Samaritan, to pick us up and carry us to healing and safety when we were helpless and stuck in our sins.
- Thank You for Your grace that allows us to start fresh each day, to walk in the good works You prepare in advance for us to walk in.

- When You call me to something hard and sacrificial, strengthen me with faith and help from the Holy Spirit to see the mission fully through.
- Thank You for punching my ticket to heaven on the cross, allowing me to be free to love my neighbors with no strings attached.

Demo Day

Remove the walls that keep you from a life of adventures with God.

What shall we say then? Are we to continue in sin that grace may abound? By no means! How can we who died to sin still live in it?

Romans 6:1–2

Cutting Corners

I am not one of those people who is constantly on the lookout for signs from God. I've never put out an actual fleece like Gideon, and I generally think that God told us everything He needed to tell us directly in the Bible. Even the promptings of the Holy Spirit that I talk about are instances when we are being led to bring to life what we've been told in the Bible in a particular moment with a particular person. So the better we know the Bible, the better we can discern God's will in the moment. Okay, I needed to put that out there, because I'm about to tell you about three freaky signs that I just can't call random coincidence. And I also want to admit up front that just because you know the Bible doesn't mean you always do the Bible.

You already know some of the backstory to this chapter, as it involves the Glen Burnie flip house and my half-Isaac offer. We had lots of time and equity wrapped up into this pretty blue rancher, and after the Grace Bomb didn't work out, we kept it on the market. We were continuing to have showings when I got another idea for a Grace Bomb. I was working with a pastor in training, whose wife and three children needed a place to stay for eighteen months before moving back to India to lead a ministry there. I thought it would be fun for them to live in our flipped house since it had a great yard for the kids and plenty of room to spread out, and we could grace bomb them with a rent lower than the mortgage. They took us up on the offer, and things were great for almost a year, until I got a call that the basement had somehow taken on water.

After a month of troubleshooting, taking up the new floor, and alas, even the new drywall, I found the culprit: an existing French drain, meant to divert water to the sump pump, had been installed incorrectly by the previous owners. The installers had literally cut corners, and as a result, moisture was beginning to come up from the ground and through the corners of the foundation. One giant mess and $10,000 later (that we didn't just have lying around in a shoebox), we had an entirely new drain put into the foundation.

The eighteen-month agreement came to an end, the family headed back to India, and we got right in to stage the house, freshen things up, and get this thing off the books, as it had become a much more expensive venture than we had planned. To say we were a little anxious to sell, after two years on a flip, was an understatement. This time around, we received multiple offers out of the gate—good offers. Everything was cruising along, until the potential buyer's home inspector flagged a possible problem with one of the basement foundation walls.

The wall in the unfinished utility room had a slight bow, probably from years of settling. It was only noticeable because of a stairstep-crack pattern in the mortar between the cinder blocks, which was visible on half of the wall. We agreed to have a third-party structural engineer come take a look and offer a solution. In the meantime, I was legit panicking. A tiny crack, which had probably been there for decades, was threatening to stop this great deal in its tracks. Nobody wants to move into a foundation problem, I figured. And how bad would the report be? Would the buyers get cold feet? Would this house ever sell?

So in a moment of lapsed judgment and integrity, I thought that maybe I could make the wall look a little less suspicious by covering it up. Not all of it—that wouldn't be very Christian of me—but just the left side of the wall and with the most obvious protrusion. I even reasoned that I could make it a possible storage feature for the new buyer—and somehow trick the engineer into giving me a clean bill of health.

I wanted to take the edge off to help our chances—a little dishonesty for the greater good—because I legitimately believed that, in all likelihood, the foundation was sound and was not a safety concern. Even though I was feeling conflicted, I had forty-eight hours before the engineer would visit, so I grabbed my tools and booked it to Home Depot for framing lumber and insulation to carry out my plan—oblivious to becoming just like the guy who had passed along the French-drain problem to me.

Third Sign's a Charm

Internally, I was a mess. I was so ready to move on from this project, and I alternately felt justified and wrong in taking matters into my own hands to deceive some people I'd never meet face to face. Deep down I knew it wasn't right, so I prayed, because I could not let go of my little scheme. And just like I don't typically look for signs, I also don't typically expect God to answer a prayer immediately—but I got both.

While en route to Home Depot, with the tools in the back of the van, I paused the country music and prayed something like "God, if You think this is a bad idea, please let me know." It was a short prayer, because just then a white Honda Civic, with an obnoxiously loud exhaust, came buzzing by in the lane to my left. This car had absolutely no conspicuous markings, except for the bumper sticker that read "666." Okay, was that a coincidence? You don't have to be a Bible expert to know that number is not a popular one. In hindsight, that seems like a relatively clear answer to prayer, but in the moment, I just kept on with the plan, picked up my supplies, then went to work on my cover-up wall.

After framing out a small portion, I noticed that I could still see most of the wall, and because of that, I figured I wasn't hiding much—just the worst part. I rationalized again that the inspector could still see behind my wall, since it wasn't totally enclosed. *I'm good*, I thought. *I'm just taking the edge off.* That feeling was fleeting, though, as I tossed and turned all night under the conviction that I shouldn't be hiding anything, period.

The next day I woke up early and started to do some work at Starbucks. Before getting into my day, I was praying about the wall I had built. I was literally writing down the question "Jesus, should I take this wall down?" in my journal when, I kid you not, at that very moment, just like Satan's Civic had driven by at the right time, the structural engineer who would inspect the house twenty-four hours later walked right through the Starbucks doors to get a coffee. This was nuts, because I live in a big county and had never seen him there before, or anywhere else for that matter. After I picked my jaw up from the floor, I resolved that, at the end of the workday, I would go do what I should have done earlier: remove the wall I had put up. I took his appearance in an unexpected place as a clear second sign, since the first one apparently hadn't been enough to get me to take action.

At the end of that day, I drove back to the house, resolved to do the right thing. But when I got to the basement and looked at my handiwork, I took a step back and thought again, *Well, the inspector can see behind the wall if he really wants to, and the buyers might want to put a corner shelf up in that spot thanks to my craftsmanship.* And I left it up.

The next morning, as I pulled into the driveway of the blue rancher, I had less than one hour before the inspector's visit. You guessed it, I was again feeling conviction that I was hiding something—because I was. So I prayed once more. I think I was really praying for strength to do what I knew was the right thing. The spirit is willing but the flesh is weak, right? Then, right there in the driveway, on a cloudy day, I closed my eyes to talk to Jesus about this one more time, as the clock was ticking. I said something like "Can You show me for real if this is a big deal?"

And then, in a very clear third sign and immediate answer to prayer, I opened my eyes to see a bright red cardinal in the middle of a cluster of overgrown vines in the backyard. It was like turning on an old black-and-white TV, except the bird was in vivid color. Seeing a cardinal might not mean much to you, but whenever Kristen or I see a red cardinal, we think about Jesus and even say "Jesus," because for some reason, that bird is a reminder of Him for us. It is our Jesus bird.

At that moment, I stopped thinking. I stopped rationalizing and debating. I jumped out of the van, grabbed my #DEMODAY hammer that Kristen bought in Waco, walked down the basement steps, and in five minutes, I had undone what I knew shouldn't have been done in the first place. I took the wall down, exposing Ol' Bow in all her glory, with about twenty minutes to spare before the engineer arrived.

I was overwhelmed that God had answered, not just one prayer, but three—immediately, and in no uncertain terms. I was humbled, actually, that God was helping me along in doing the right thing with a silly little real-estate deal. Although there were billions of other people on the planet, many with far greater problems, He was taking time for me, because He wanted more for me. He wanted me to feel His peace that comes after fully trusting Him. And that is exactly what happened. All my anxiety about losing the real-estate deal melted away the moment I swung that hammer, because even if I lost the deal, I knew I was gaining a closer walk with God—and it felt great.

There are lots of reasons we rationalize, justify, and excuse the times that we choose not to walk in God's expressed will for us. When that happens, we put up walls that become barriers in our relationship with Him. These walls tell God, "I don't fully trust You to take care of what is on the other side of the wall." We figure that somehow, if He tells us do something, He might not have our best interests in mind. These flesh-born blockades prevent us from carrying out His will, hearing clearly from Him, and walking in the good works that He has prepared for us to walk in. It is difficult to listen to the promptings of the Holy Spirit when we are stiff-arming Him in other areas of our lives.

God's desire is not to leave these walls standing, but to help us take them down, opening us up to His peace and provision. And that, friends, is the prime launching pad for many Grace Bombing adventures. His help might come in the form of a timely answered prayer, a Satan Civic, a Jesus bird, or a timely rebuke. The latter was the case for one famous king who needed to get back on track after building an epic wall.

David's Epic Wall

You'd recognize David from the time he defeated a giant named Goliath with a slingshot. This was the fight that hurled him into the public spotlight for his bravery and trust in God, and he went on to become a well-known military leader and the second king to preside over the unified nation of Israel. He took the reins from King Saul, who had lost his ability to govern after pulling his own half-Isaac. Then David eventually turned the kingdom over to his son Solomon. David had many victories as king, and God even described him as a "man after his [God's] own heart" (1 Sam. 13:14).

King David was a giant slayer, an underdog, a poet, and a prophet who left a significantly godly wake. But at the same time, he was also known for one of the most epic fails in history—when he went for the record of how many commandments could be broken all at once, in turn triggering a legacy of violence.

It was springtime, the time when kings would lead their troops to secure borders, drive out intruders, and keep the peace by enforcing military strength. The problem this particular spring was that David sent his troops out to battle while he stayed home. We don't know why. Maybe he was tired or stressed out. Whatever the reason, shrugging off his responsibilities that season gave way to a great temptation. The account reads, "It happened, late one afternoon, when David arose from his couch and was walking on the roof of the king's house, that he saw from the roof a woman bathing; and the woman was very beautiful. And David sent and inquired about the woman" (2 Sam. 11:2–3).

Here was the most powerful guy in the land strolling on the balcony of the penthouse, and he saw a beautiful woman in the shower at the house nearby. What could possibly go wrong? He sent for her, even after it was clear that she was a married woman. Even worse, she was married to Uriah, a good soldier in David's army. What happened next was an ancient example of the reason the #MeToo movement exists today. David leveraged his power to use Bathsheba as an object of his lust. Later, David learned that this sexual encounter had resulted in Bathsheba becoming pregnant with his child. And from that point on, the story reads like Jerry Springer and the Knights of the Round Table.

When David heard the news of Bathsheba's pregnancy, he did what most people in power who mess up do—he tried to cover it up. I mean, who am I to blame him? I tried to cover up a few cracks in a wall. He was the military and spiritual leader of a nation who had just betrayed both trusts simultaneously by disrespecting God's clear commands and those under his command. It took three attempts for David to cover his tracks.

If David could convince Bathsheba's husband, Uriah, to hurry up and sleep with his wife, then it might appear as if the child was Uriah's own, as they were still millennia away from paternity testing. So David brought Uriah in from the field to try to convince him to go home and spend some time with his wife. This deception backfired when Uriah honorably declined to leave his brothers-in-arms behind on the battlefield, making Uriah more heroic and David more pathetic.

David tried the same scheme a second time, on this attempt having Uriah party for a while and get a little tipsy, hoping that alcohol would lower his inhibitions enough to go home and have relations with Bathsheba. But Uriah's loyalty was the stronger spirit, and he never went home that night. Little did Uriah know that, in his commitment to David and the kingdom, he was signing his own death sentence.

With the maternity clock already ticking away, David's third attempt for a cover-up was a more permanent solution. He would have Uriah killed and then marry Bathsheba as a merciful public gesture. This would seemingly make the child a legitimate son, with much less suspicion as to the time of conception. Of course, Uriah's death would have to look like an accident—a situation that David planned for and saw carried out. Before long, the deed was done, the cover-up complete, and life could go on as usual—or so he thought.

A Timely Rebuke

Clearly, God was not cool with what went down. David had lost his mind, and "the thing that David had done displeased the LORD" (2 Sam. 11:27). God's patience does have holy limits, as can be seen at other times when He calls "time's up" on evil and injustice. But here again, God dropped a Grace Bomb, not a lightning bolt. He did so by simply calling out the truth in a way that broke David's heart, eventually causing the wall between them to crumble. God dropped a much-needed rebuke on David.

Enter the prophet Nathan, whom David already knew and had confided in. He approached David and told a story that, for all David knew, was a real-time provincial case that needed judgment. Nathan said:

> There were two men in a certain city, the one rich and the other poor. The rich man had very many flocks and herds, but the poor man had nothing but one little ewe lamb, which he had bought. And he brought it up, and it grew up with him and with his children. It used to eat of his morsel and drink from his cup and lie in his arms, and it was like a daughter to him. Now there came a traveler to the rich man, and he was unwilling to take one of his own flock or herd to prepare for the guest who had come to him, but he took the poor man's lamb and prepared it for the man who had come to him. (2 Sam. 12:1–4)

This is a messed-up little story about greed, exploitation, entitlement, insensitivity, and carelessness, all packaged inside of a petting zoo. It would make for a great Netflix series. It's a clever story, especially given David's shepherding background, to help him see his sin in a new light. The story triggered in David a visceral response, as the text reads:

> Then David's anger was greatly kindled against the man, and he said to Nathan, "As the LORD lives, the man who has done this deserves to die, and he shall restore the lamb fourfold, because he did this thing, and because he had no pity." (vv. 5–6)

Fully bought in, David not only felt the emotion of the tale but also decided the retribution and sentencing of this man. This guy deserved to die, and the poor man was owed a great debt. Only, the story actually had nothing to do with sheep, but represented David's stealing, lying, adultery, and murder. Nathan delivered the swift strike to the heart: "You are the man!" (v. 7), and then he made it clear that David had despised God's Word and chosen to carry out a great evil (vv. 8–12).

Through this timely rebuke, David's eyes were opened to reality, and he came to the vulnerable place of a contrite heart and genuine repentance. And while the gravity of his actions had lingering negative consequences for his family and beyond, his relationship with God was restored, and he was able to walk in God's purposes again.

Let me put it another way. With so much mess between himself and God, David wasn't grace bombing people to the degree that God intended. Until David owned his sin, confessed it, and turned his life completely back over to God, he would stay in a funk. That's why Nathan was a gift. That's why taking one square on the chin from God's Word can snap us back to a better reality.

Nathan Lives

Nathan is alive and well today. Well, not that Nathan, but our
Nathan. Back then, the prophet communicated God's truth and
desires directly to David, while today God's Word speaks with that
same authority. We are told that "all Scripture is breathed out by
God and profitable for teaching, for reproof, for correction, and for
training in righteousness, that the man of God may be complete,
equipped for every good work" (2 Tim. 3:16–17). That means that
when God gives us clear instructions, we should always shoot for a
full-Isaac—and to walk in those instructions that have in mind our
good and God's glory.

For example, in his letter to the Ephesians, after explaining that
we are grace-built people given a purpose to grace bomb people,
Paul urged us to walk in a manner worthy of this calling and posi-
tion. He went into detail about how to walk in love and integrity, as
he called us to choose honesty over lying (Eph. 4:25), work harder
instead of stealing (v. 28), use our words to build others up instead
of tearing them down (v. 29), be kind and tender instead of being
angry and bitter (vv. 26, 31), guard our sex lives and keep them
pure (5:3), guard our hearts from coveting what others have and be
content (v. 5), and be filled by God rather than controlled by other
substances (v. 18), to name a few of the best ways God says to live.

These commands are not the rules of a religion but the char-
acteristics of a relationship. They are born out of God's own holy
nature and will for our lives—that we should be a royal priesthood
and a holy nation of Grace Bombers who can live free from walls
between us and God.

But as I said earlier, you can know the Bible and not always do the Bible. Thankfully, when we do put up walls, God gives us the ability to grab our #DEMODAY hammers and get back on track with Him. This is a routine practice in the life of a Grace Bomber who will frequently come back to the starting place of grace.

Demo Day

Everybody loves demo day, when the old walls come down to make room for a new way to live. Repentance is like that. It's taking action by turning from the old ways of stiff-arming God and opening ourselves to something new—in faith that the new thing really is the better thing. After Nathan called him out, David wrote Psalm 51, my go-to blueprint for how to talk to God and trust Him when it's time to make a change: we own it, God takes it, and joy is renewed.

Everybody loves demo day, when the old walls come down to make room for a new way to live. Repentance is like that.

While the entire psalm is beneficial, I want to show you how I pray through it after I blow it, in the hopes that this will give you a practical way to respond to the times when Nathan comes knocking at your door.

We Own It

> Have mercy on me, O God,
>> according to your steadfast love;
> according to your abundant mercy
>> blot out my transgressions.
> Wash me thoroughly from my iniquity,
>> and cleanse me from my sin!
>
> For I know my transgressions,
>> and my sin is ever before me.
> Against you, you only, have I sinned
>> and done what is evil in your sight. (Ps. 51:1–4)

Right out of the gate, remember that God is for you. His love is steadfast; it holds up in the storm. We may think we have reasons to call that into question, such as when the circumstances of life are terrible or we've suffered great loss. But when we talk to God, we must presume that He actually does love us and is for us.

This is especially important as we begin to consider our sins. Just look at how many times words for *sin* are repeated in this passage: *transgressions, iniquity, sin, transgressions, sin, sinned, evil.* Yikes! Sounds like what you'd hear if you played a heavy-metal song backward. This is absolute exposure and vulnerability and can be one of the most difficult things for any person to face—to own the fact that, in light of a perfect moral being, we have blown it big time. But it is actually a gift to see this in ourselves.

Step one, own it. Be vulnerable and be exposed. And like David, keep in mind that, while sin is not great for us or others, it is primarily against God Himself. While in building my wall I may have been dishonest with an inspector or future home buyer, I was first telling God that I didn't trust Him and wanted to handle the situation my own way. It's like saying to the inventor of life that you know how to do life better; and when that happens, we overstep His boundaries.

God Takes It

> Purge me with hyssop, and I shall be clean;
> wash me, and I shall be whiter than snow.
> Let me hear joy and gladness;
> let the bones that you have broken rejoice.
> Hide your face from my sins,
> and blot out all my iniquities.
> Create in me a clean heart, O God,
> and renew a right spirit within me. (Ps. 51:7–10)

David understood that his guilt and shame needed to be put somewhere. He could only look forward to the time when God would make a final cleansing act to justly lift the stain of sin from the human soul by placing it on Jesus. We have the advantage over David to know the whole story and look back in full detail to that event. Even so, David understood that God forgives. It is His heavy lifting that makes things right. God is the heart-cleaner. God renews a right spirit. God creates a new birth and a fresh start.

Step two, hand it over at the cross. This is where God does business with our walls, and this is where He cleans up our debris. Ask Him, like David did, to create in you a clean heart. Ask Him for a new heart, with new desires, and a new bandwidth for trust.

Walk in Joy

> Restore to me the joy of your salvation,
>   and uphold me with a willing spirit.
>
> Then I will teach transgressors your ways,
>   and sinners will return to you. (Ps. 51:12–13)

The great outcome of doing the hard soul work—of receiving Nathan's rebuke in the nooks and crannies of our lives, of taking those things to heart as serious matters of holiness, of owning and calling it out in ourselves, and then crying out in thankfulness for the provision of forgiveness through Jesus—is in one word, *joy*.

Joy is the experience that flows from an unhindered relationship with God. We were put on this planet to enjoy Him. This is the joy of fulfilling our highest purpose in this life, to know and walk with our Creator. The best of life will flow out of this relationship, as will all of the other good works He has prepared for us to walk in. To that end, notice that it was after David was restored that he went on to be an influence for the Lord.

In Psalm 51, David walked us through the anatomy of a demo day: having a contrite heart, making an honest confession, accepting total forgiveness, and then joyfully emerging ready for action. Perhaps you need to follow suit if Nathan has called you "the man" anywhere in the book so far.

Maybe you can identify with Gideon's fear. Or you find yourself avoiding Samaritans or just being a bad Samaritan. Maybe you're settling for half-Isaacs or spotting some walls that you don't intend to demo anytime soon. If this is you, believe me I get it, and I encourage you to own it, hand it over, and get ready to walk in joy. Life is so much better when the walls between us and God come down.

Growing in Grace Bombing impact requires identifying the walls that are actively keeping you from loving people or hearing clearly from the Holy Spirit. Sometimes these walls can just spring up overnight, after you visit Home Depot for supplies. As these parts of your life become more evident, you now know the practical steps of a healthy practice of demo day to deal with them. Swing away with the Carpenter's hammer, and find yourself ready to follow in the footsteps of the Master Bomber.

Depth Charge

Heavenly Father:

- Thank You that You are patient with me when I clearly begin to tune You out and make decisions that put things between us.
- Thank You that even today I have Your helpful and practical Word that clearly expresses Your will for certain areas of my life. Create in me a deep, spiritual hunger to know it.
- Empower me to own the walls I have put up, to repent and take them down, and then to be set free to walk with You in the newness of life.
- Help me, Lord, to cast off those things that can so easily prevent me from hearing from You and keep me from grace bombing my neighbor.

Part Three

Supernatural Fuel Supply

A New Love

Explode with newness by finding the freedom of unconditional love.

We love because he first loved us.

1 John 4:19

There Is No Spoon

When *The Matrix* came out back in 1999, my mind was blown. The movie depicted a small group of people who had learned the truth about their reality—they had been living in a computer simulation, the Matrix, designed by artificial intelligence to keep the human race subservient. Once they escaped from the Matrix, they worked to free others and undermine the power of the simulation.

If you have seen this watershed film, you might recall a scene where Neo, played by Keanu Reeves, pays a visit to Oracle, a sort of all-knowing character who can tell him the deeper purposes of his life and reveal truths about his destiny. Neo, who recently broke free from the Matrix, finds himself in Oracle's living room, along with others waiting to see her. There he meets a little boy, sitting on the floor, bending a spoon with his mind—really hard to do; I've tried. Neo leans in, intrigued. Here is the dialogue that follows:

Spoon Boy: Do not try and bend the spoon. That's impossible. Instead, only try to realize the truth.

Neo: What truth?

Spoon Boy: There is no spoon.

In the world of *The Matrix*, there literally was no spoon. It was generated by the computer simulation, something your mind believed to be there. Today, lots of God-fearing people in the world have one particular religious spoon. But it's not actually a spoon; it's a scale—a heavenly scale held by God Himself upon which they believe He measures out our good and bad. If you were to stop people on the street who believe in God and ask them how people get into heaven, most would paint this kind of picture:

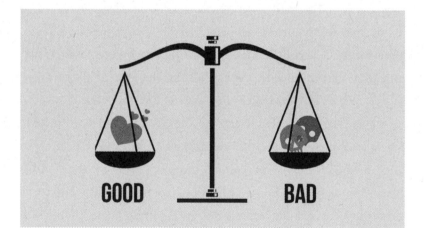

Simply put, if by the time I kick the bucket my good deeds outweigh my bad deeds, then I've got a good shot of God accepting me and ending up in the "good" place. This is the basic framework for most of the world's major religions, outside of biblical Christianity. But in the words of Spoon Boy, I would say, "Do not try to tip the heavenly scale. That's impossible. Instead, only try to realize the truth. There is no scale."

Do not try to tip the heavenly scale. That's impossible. Instead, only try to realize the truth. There is no scale.

In a book that can help you get started on an adventure of generously fun investments in your neighbors, I want to be clear that the point is not to try to fill up a heavenly scale that will get us on God's good side. Earning God's good graces by tipping the scale had been my wife's mind-set until a series of events led her to see that there is no scale—but something far better. To dig in, we need to revisit the time two kids from Maryland fell in love and then found a love they weren't expecting.

The Notebook

Kristen and I met in high school. She was the hot athlete girl in all the smart classes—way out of my league by a long shot. I wasn't a varsity jock or a smart kid, and I had zero game with the ladies. I didn't even know there was a game, which somehow must have made it seem like I had game. Later in life, I heard that my mysterious vibe was really helping my cause, even though I was clueless at the time. High school girls might have thought that when I was staring off into space I was pondering the existential realities of the universe, but I was probably just thinking about what I could burn in the woods after school.

So clearly, by some mistake with Old Mill High administration, Kristen and I ended up having a class together. From there, we shared the same lunch table from time to time. But it was not until our senior year, when I went to a tennis match where Kristen was playing solo—tennis skirt and all—opening a can of whoop on her opponent, that my eyes were opened and I realized that I needed to get some game, and fast.

It wasn't long after that day that we found ourselves holding hands in the metal bleachers at a school lacrosse game and then driving to Chick and Ruth's deli on Main Street in Annapolis for our first date. I ordered a big breakfast plate; she had oatmeal. It didn't matter that it was well past dinner time; neither of us ate much. I'm not even sure how I paid for it. I probably borrowed some money from my dad.

That started an epic summer of falling for each other; although, to our parents it was probably more like falling into a problem. Our friends also started to wonder where in the world we went. In the words of the rapping blues artist G. Love, I didn't "get out to see the boys anymore … they think I'm on some extended vacation."[1] We had welded on love goggles and tried to spend as much time together in bodies of water as possible, probably because we looked really good in bathing suits.

But a Loch Ness Monster was lurking in the waters of our newfound infatuation, a monster called college, and it was bearing down fast. Kristen had plans to go off to St. Francis University in Pennsylvania, which was a solid three hours away from where I was headed. Three hours away in college is like measuring distance in dog years, so I might as well have been living on another planet.

It felt like we were living that movie, *The Notebook*—a summer fling where two young people end up smitten yet doomed for failure, as she goes off to a fancy college to be wooed by new and cultured experiences, and he pines away back home in a small town—except nobody romantically dies at the end. My hometown of Glen Burnie is a place that proves time travel is possible, as you can quickly find yourself back in 1985, a magical time when mullets and Trans Ams run free with no judgment—and you don't need a DeLorean to get there.

But eventually, we got to the business of making life on different planets work. For the better part of those college years, we wrote letters that required postage, since texting wasn't a thing yet, logged lots of miles on ill-advised visits through sketchy winter storms, had some great times, and made the most of every holiday and break. We gave it the old college try! But there was also some *stuff*. It wouldn't be *The Notebook*, after all, without some drama and heartache. But none of that really came to light, until Kristen moved back home.

Howl at the Moon

Kristen moved back to Maryland for her fifth year of college, as she jumped straight into her master's program, and it seemed as though the old gang was going to rise, like a phoenix from the ashes. Had we really survived four years of a long-distance young-adult romance?

At the time, I was wondering that myself, when we happened to run into some high school friends who had recently heard about the Jesus of the Bible and were now following Him wholeheartedly. Lori and Sarah had been good friends with Kristen, and they too were a couple of those athletic, smart kids that outclassed me be a mile. But I knew they were more than just cool kids; they were legendary party kids. Regular party kids go home after a party; legendary party kids go missing after parties and somehow turn back up in class on Monday. This made it even more weird that they were now following Jesus.

When we bumped into Sarah at the gym, she invited us to come hang out at the Howl at the Moon Café, a dueling-piano bar in downtown Baltimore. No-brainer. Shouting over the blasting pianos, she told us that we should check out her small-group Bible study that Lori was helping lead on Wednesday nights. This invitation was a harder sell, not knowing what kind of kooky stuff would be going on, but we went. Honestly, we were expecting either a bunch of Christian bookworms or freaks passing out Kool-Aid waiting for the Hale-Bopp comet to fly by.

I was suspicious about that first visit but was pleasantly surprised to meet the small group of young professionals, who seemed to be doing well in life and were not at all awkward to be around. If anything, I was the awkward one. One guy, named Mike, was particularly disarming, as he sat on the floor, while everyone else was in a chair or sofa, and busted jokes most of the time.

This was my first exposure to people my age reading and making applications of the Bible together and really taking Jesus seriously. I knew deep down that this was something missing for me—this strange kind of community that was helping one another walk with

Jesus in everyday life. I mean, I had faith in Jesus growing up. I believed that He was God's Son who came into the world to die on a cross to save people from their sins. But church had become nothing more than a family routine, and my faith practices were largely limited to attending services on Sundays.

I remember going to the Church of the Advent, an Episcopal church located in South Baltimore, and reciting words that I didn't always mean and keeping my church life very separate from my private life—Great Wall of China separate. In fact, I vividly remember kneeling down and praying to "serve and please [God] in the newness of life" while simultaneously thinking *but not really because there is a big party tomorrow night, and I'm 'bout to get my buzz on.* Given our tendency to seek out ways to wear bathing suits, we were not winning any gold medals for purity in our dating relationship—another reason I didn't truthfully pray that prayer.

But God was patient with me—He knew when I was faking it. At that point in my life, He knew I was more excited to be controlled by a substance, or my hormones, than by Him. Through this graceful chain of events, He was drawing back a prodigal son, opening my eyes to a new desire to want to live in the "newness of life." Meanwhile, Kristen was being drawn to something bigger too, something seismic. For her, Mike, who always seemed to be sitting on the floor, might as well have been bending spoons with his mind, as she would soon learn, there is no spoon.

The Second Wednesday Night

It was just the second Wednesday night visiting the Bible study when something drastically changed in Kristen's mind and heart.

Like me, she had grown up in a religious home, with lots of repetitive activity, but she knew very little about Jesus as a real person who could offer real help. She had never personally opened a Bible and had not yet been led to draw her own conclusions about whether Jesus really was historically who He claimed to be, or if He is simply a product of mythology that gives people a beneficial moral framework.

But that had not stopped her from going through the motions of Sunday school, first Communion, confirmation, and other ordinances of the church as prescribed by family tradition. I did all of those things too—but even more so for Kristen, Jesus stayed tightly confined to those boxes. She equated Jesus with the religion that can be so easily built around Him. It's like she had a treasure in a box, but the box was never opened up and the treasure never enjoyed. And while she might not have been able to articulate it at the time, carrying around the box of religion was quite heavy, quite burdensome. Yet she did, because in her mind that would likely help tip the scales in her favor, as she sought to earn God's love for her.

Then the disruptive message of grace came rushing in like a stream of living water on scorched earth. Sitting in a carpeted living room in a town house with a bunch of young adults, Kristen heard straight from the Bible itself that there is no divine scale. Instead, it was only the good works that Jesus did that could change our standing before God—and this was simply a love gift, a Grace Bomb.

This spiritual truth cut through all the noise of regular life, as Sarah and Lori explained this "good news" about Jesus' free, "no strings attached," personal love for Kristen that she did not have to earn. It was an emotional moment (she balled her eyes out—the ugly cry), and right then, she seemed to experience a real spiritual change that would lead to more practical changes in the days that followed.

What Kristen heard that night was a lot like what another religious person heard directly from Jesus Himself. Nicodemus was one of the most religious people you could meet during the lifetime of Jesus and was simultaneously clueless about how getting close to God really worked. Jesus blew his mind by informing Him there was no spoon—no heavenly scale. This had to be a shocker, because he had probably spent most of his life trying to bend it.

Nic at Night

Nicodemus was a Pharisee and likely a member of a group of rulers among them, known as the Sanhedrin. He was sincere, devout, pious, and an amazing religious rule keeper. His mind-set was like Kristen's was growing up, as well as like that of many well-meaning religious people today: that God will love and accept me if I am a good person, keep His rules, and try not to break His commandments; but if I do, hopefully it won't be bad enough to tip the scales in the wrong direction permanently.

Nicodemus had real questions about who Jesus was. He was seeking light, as opposed to some other Pharisees who had already made up their minds about Jesus. Nicodemus had either seen or heard of the supernatural signs that Jesus was performing. And as signs are supposed to do, they were pointing Nicodemus to something bigger: the true identity of Jesus. He wasn't able to see that yet, but that would eventually change.

The conversation happened at night, possibly up on a rooftop. For most people who are not insomniacs or mafiosos, it is neither convenient nor socially acceptable to schedule meetings at night. But the value of a nighttime meeting is that it helps keep the meeting hidden from others.

As a prominent religious ruler, whose Pharisee peers were not exactly Jesus' biggest fans, Nicodemus wasn't ready to be seen publicly taking an interest in Jesus, not ready to break ranks with the status quo. He was following Jesus on social media but definitely not dropping any likes. Personally, I get it. It can be easy to be into Jesus privately, but displaying that devotion out in the open is a whole different matter, especially when your friends would not be cool with it.

Nicodemus respectfully started the conversation this way: "Rabbi, we know that you are a teacher come from God, for no one can do these signs that you do unless God is with him" (John 3:2).

Jesus didn't address the signs, per se; instead, as usual, He cut through the small talk to the heart of Nicodemus' problem: "Truly, truly, I say to you, unless one is born again he cannot see the kingdom of God" (v. 3). Jesus clarified the requirements for heaven—a new birth, not good deeds.

Now, can we admit for a second that the phrase "born again" has gotten a bad rap? It might stir up a cultish vibe of some odd Christian subculture that's going to pop up as a new Netflix miniseries, or incite visceral feelings about pushy church people who are way too zealous about their faith. But the phrase was not invented by any church, or church people for that matter, but by Jesus Himself— and considering the master teacher that He was, it's actually a very helpful phrase.

To be "born again" was Nicodemus' greatest need and greatest misunderstanding. It was his greatest need because he couldn't have heaven without this spiritual condition. It was his greatest misunderstanding because his supposed divine scale could not bring about a new birth. The scale involves work that people do, but a person cannot give birth to himself. The very phrase, "born again," engenders a complete dependence upon someone other than self.

This was obviously problematic for Nicodemus. He was a rule follower, and dependence upon someone else was nowhere on his list of boxes to check. His worldview saw his good works putting him in a better standing with God, not being "born again." Into Nicodemus' confusion, Jesus pushed back that, as a teacher of Israel's law, Nicodemus should not have been surprised by the need for a heart- and soul-level change in a person.[2] But Jesus didn't leave it at this loving rebuke; instead, He worked with what Nicodemus did know and connected the dots for him through one sentence that explains exactly how one becomes born again to see the kingdom of God.

Just Look Up

Nicodemus knew the history of the Israelites, and in one sentence that referenced a weird story about killer snakes, Jesus helped him crack the code of how one became born again. Jesus explained, "And as Moses lifted up the serpent in the wilderness, so must the Son of Man be lifted up, that whoever believes in him may have eternal life" (John 3:14–15). I know that sounds totally strange to us, but let me explain, because it made total sense to Nicodemus.

Nicodemus knew the story Jesus was talking about from Numbers 21 in the Old Testament. The Israelites were rebelling against God and Moses, as they traveled as nomads in the wilderness. Grumbling and cursing, they complained about God's provision for them. This aroused God's righteous wrath against them, and He sent to the camp "fiery serpents" that bit and killed the people. If that sounds harsh or unfair, keep in mind who exactly the Israelites were offending: God Himself, the Holy Creator, who only had their best interest in mind. And when God makes a judgment, it is always the right call.

The people responded by repenting of their affront to God's provision for them and turning back toward Moses. After Moses prayerfully interceded for them, God told him the remedy for those bitten and dying: "Make a fiery serpent and set it on a pole, and everyone who is bitten, when he sees it, shall live" (Num. 21:8).

Make a snake, lift it up, and tell the people to look. Weird, but effective, because it was what God did to save the people. He didn't tell the people to scramble for the antivenom or to try to heap a bunch of good works on the scale to hold back certain death, but instead, only to look up. Because in looking up they were trusting in the right object of God's salvation. By looking at the bronze serpent, they were putting their full faith and confidence in what God said would save them. It signified turning back to God in faith. This was the picture Jesus wanted in Nicodemus' mind when He then added, "So must the Son of Man be lifted up, that whoever believes in him may have eternal life" (John 3:14–15).

"Son of Man" was one of Jesus' favorites in referring to Himself (Dan. 7:13). Being "lifted up" referred to His death on the cross. So Jesus leveraged this Old Testament story that Nicodemus immediately understood to identify Jesus Himself as the object of faith that led to salvation, or to being born again. To look to Jesus is to trust the provision that God made for forgiveness and salvation, at which point a great transaction occurs—He removes sin and replaces it with His righteousness and the gift of the Holy Spirit, causing a soul that was previously dead to God to come alive (Eph. 2:1–4), or as Jesus said it, to be born again.

While we seem to be given just the highlights of the conversation that night, I could imagine Jesus saying something like this: "There you go, Nicodemus. There's the answer to your deepest questions. I know you're pretty religious, so tell Me, which rules do you believe are going to make God save you? Is it the food laws you must obey? Is it the amount of money you put in the offering? Is it by serving the poor and caring for the widows? Is it praying at the temple three times a day or making the pilgrimage to the holy places? No, man. On all accounts, no. It's not by doing good things, Nicodemus. Your performance can never change your spiritual brokenness. Instead, I must be lifted up, on a cross. I must settle your account of sin and then freely give you this new status of being made alive to God. Your job, Nicodemus, is to believe in Me. Nic, here is the deal— the only way to God is through God and you are looking at Him. Nicodemus, throw away your scale and just trust Me."

At some point, he did. Nicodemus resurfaced two more times in John's gospel after this conversation, and it appears that he turned in his scale for the gift of God's grace in Jesus. Nicodemus wanted to love Jesus back. In fact, out of a thankful heart he brought a gift to honor Jesus in His death: seventy-five pounds of myrrh and aloes to be used in wrapping Jesus' body after His crucifixion—an extremely expensive gift that showed Nicodemus openly identifying with Jesus (John 19:39). This man who met with Jesus to inquire about His "signs" discovered the point of those signs: the revelation of the divinity of Jesus, who came in love to save people, without first weighing their good works.

Things begin to change after the gift of grace changes you. Since our souls are invisible, and regeneration[3] is invisible, only God knows if someone is truly reborn. Like the wind, it might not be visible to our eyes, but we can feel its effects. One indicator that a person has been rebuilt by grace is a new desire to want to love Jesus back and obey Him regardless of the cost.

The Gold Volvo

Kristen heard nothing of Moses, snakes on poles, or Nicodemus that night, but she did hear of Jesus who loved her even when she wasn't keeping any of His rules. Upon hearing that, she looked up, let go of the scale, and embraced her Savior. I'll never forget it—the tears of joy, the laughter, the loving support in the room. There was nothing fake or overemotionalized, nothing sketchy or cultish, just a holy moment when someone's prayers were being answered. The gospel had just obliterated Kristen's religious check boxes, and now she wanted to embrace the treasure and live a life that says "thanks." It didn't take long to see the effects of this change, blowing across the unsettled waters of our relationship. And I needed to buckle up.

One of those Wednesday nights, which quickly became a routine, I drove Kristen home in the same gold Volvo we used on our first date some five years earlier. Kristen said we needed to talk, because toward the end of college, some things had gone unspoken about the status of our relationship. Now you might be thinking that college is usually a time of debauchery, mixed with discovery, and it's not like you guys were married! True that, but pain is pain, and drama is drama, and what I had thought our relationship was, for a time, wasn't.

Kristen told me that, during the last year of college, she was dating another guy pretty seriously while we were still together-ish. I hadn't known the extent of the relationship until that moment—and it absolutely sucked to hear about it. I had figured now that she was back in Maryland, we'd just fall back into the summer romance that had started it all off. But she put it all out there, pulling a skeleton out of the closet, to say thanks to Jesus.

The Holy Spirit, taking up residence in her regenerated soul, had begun to spotlight some areas of concern. Some of her moral areas, which previously were fifty shades of gray, were now becoming black and white. To her credit, she wanted to address them as matters of right and wrong. She could have kept those secrets, but instead, she rolled the dice of confession and brought the hard things into the light.

Kristen wanted to give Jesus a gift of honesty and integrity, even if that meant this bad news would end our relationship. Yes, sometimes saying thanks to Jesus will require taking a relational 2x4 to the head of someone you love. On the hood of the car, with my jaw still on the ground, Kristen put Jesus ahead of everything else—even her own happiness, assuming I might be a source of that for her, especially because that other relationship had already ended.

Now I can't tell you that I didn't repress some thoughts over the years or that I never internalized the stress or cursed sorority life or had my insecurities play out in bad dreams of beating people up—fights I always won by the way. But I can tell you what I really believed I was seeing before my eyes. I was seeing a new creation learning to walk. I was seeing a young woman putting Jesus first. I was seeing the hot girl from the tennis court wanting to walk in newness of life. I was seeing an honest moment that was honoring God. I was seeing Kristen living a thankful life based on the new gift of grace she had received. She did the next right thing and left the outcome up to Jesus.

In those weeks of my own faith being rekindled through the small group, and with God's grace on such amazing display, my heart was being prepared for this news. While Kristen was being led to be honest, I was being led to say, "You are forgiven." It was like Jesus was asking me this: "Do you really believe that My grace makes people new? Do you really believe I can change people? If the answer is yes, you can completely trust this girl again." So He enabled me to drop a Grace Bomb on Kristen in the form of forgiveness, of not keeping score, and of not holding up a divine scale in her face. In that moment, I felt no hard feelings but actually an excitement to start something new with this new creation.

In many ways, that night on the hood of the Volvo was the place a new relationship was born—when two people were deciding that Jesus should come first and that obeying Him was a really good idea. Less than two years later, we took another right step in getting married, and seventeen years and four kids later, our favorite way to say "you are forgiven" is still "grace abounds." Trust me, we need it, as there are still plenty of times when we need to hit the reset button.

And for all of us who need to get back on track, grace abounds with Jesus. He is the one who places new desires in our hearts and who is able to change us from the inside out. He is the one who removes the burden of religious performance, the one who tells us there is no spoon. Bending your mind around that grace changes everything and then frees you to bend that grace toward your neighbors.

Explosive Force

A person born again in Christ becomes an explosive force for constructive change. Just look at the many ways this newness of life has the ability to impact you—and then radiate as light to others. Some of these changes I've touched on already; others I'll explain a little further in our final chapter together.

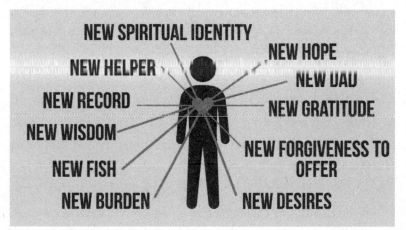

A renewed heart that has been made alive in Christ forges a brand-new *spiritual identity*. I'll explore this more in the final chapter, but it simply means that we are new creations in Christ and find our true identity in God's view of us.

This gives us *new hope*—both for now and for the future. We have a living hope, that for all eternity we will live face to face with

God in holy perfection. In addition, we have hope in God's promises to bring about good in our lives today, even when the days are hard and painful.

To remind us of these blessings, we have a *new helper*, the Holy Spirit, now taking residence in our souls as a comforter, guide, and tailwind in daily living.

He reminds us that we have a *new dad*—not to diminish our earthly dads and the lessons they taught us, for better or worse, but to recognize that we are loved and cared for perfectly by a heavenly Father, who is unchanging and always working in the best interests of His children.

When He opens the file folder of our souls, we have a *new record* that includes no documentation of our sins, as they have been removed as far as the east is from the west. God stopped keeping score and then erased the files.

This wells up in us a *new gratitude*, not only for the removal of wrongs, but also for the providential care that we are given each day—if we are mindful to dwell on such things. A thankful heart is a potent remedy to drive the dark clouds of despair out of our lives.

With this bright clarity, the *new wisdom* we have been given can be readily accessed. This wisdom includes not only the answers to the deepest questions that human beings are asking today, such as "Why are we here?" or "What's the purpose of my life?" but also daily common sense to make life more stable, secure, and enjoyable.

Our new hearts lead us to offer a *new forgiveness* to those who hurt us. It is hard to give what you don't have, but a forgiven heart can bend grace to another. We are even told to forgive others because we have been forgiven.

The new life also gives us *new fish* to fry. Jesus calls those who are forgiven and made new to get in the game of fishing for men and women. He calls us to pursue souls that have yet to come alive to God so they can be restored to the ultimate purpose of their lives: to be in a relationship with Him.

This is now our *new burden*. No longer is there a burden of religious rule keeping, earning or working to merit God's good graces, but there is a new, deep, soulful desire to see other dry bones come alive.

This is just one of many *new desires* that become heaven's marching orders in our lives. These holy desires range from the intimate and personal to the bold and public, all of them together forging a life of explosive impact for the giver, who is also the receiver of the amazing grace that caused all these things to become new.

There is no force in the universe stronger than God's personal and soul-satisfying love for you. It is spiritual gravity, a law that holds all other realities in place. When you wrap your arms around those that are outstretched toward you, with wholehearted trust, you are grounded yet able to fly, stable but explosive, a weapon of mass construction. You are freed and can now live to free others, bursting forth with grace and truth.

Depth Charge

Heavenly Father:

- Thank You that Your love for me is unconditional.
- Teach me to live freely and without pressure to earn Your good graces.
- Thank You for Jesus who died on the cross to save me from my sins.
- Allow me to absorb Your grace and bend it toward others today and every day.

Fury Unleashed

Refuel your generosity by resting in the riches of what God has already provided.

> *... having the eyes of your heart enlightened, that you may*
> *know what is the hope to which he has called you, what are the*
> *riches of his glorious inheritance in the saints, and what is the*
> *immeasurable greatness of his power toward us who believe.*
>
> Ephesians 1:18–19

Cut Me, Mick

Let me take you back to life just after our Volvo-hood confessional. Relationally, it was an exciting time. Kristen and I were back on and moving forward with a new lease on life, cosigned by Jesus. We were learning new things from the Bible study and excited to put them into practice in real life with some new friends. But internally, I was battling a real identity crisis. What might sound superficial was a big struggle that led to a drastic maneuver for a twenty-two-year-old kid.

Out of high school and into college, I got into the relatively small acting market in the Baltimore/DC area. I never hit stardom, because I can't act, but I did get a lot of auditions because I had a "look." Now, I'm no Brad Pitt, but I wouldn't get picked last in the good-looking kickball game either, if you're picking up what I'm putting down. I was told, as a young boy, that I was cute, and even remember hairdressers at the mall debating if I could be a model or not. One voted yes, the other voted no and told me I needed to start using conditioner and take better care of my skin. I was probably thirteen at the time and had never heard of conditioner until that day. My lack of hygiene aside, it felt good to hear people think I was attractive, and plus, that sounded like an easy way to make money. Blue steel, *cha-ching*.[1] It also fueled an undercurrent of pridefully wanting to disprove the haters.

Debates aside, I managed to land the occasional regional commercial and even got to play a bad guy with a few lines on *America's Most Wanted*, a guy who they later caught by the way—you're welcome, America. But instead of pointing fingers at my lack of memorization and believability, I instead pointed to my least favorite facial feature: my big, dangly, protruding, round earlobes. If you have ever obsessed about changing something about yourself, that was me.

I was convinced my ears were the exact problem and that if they could get "fixed," nothing would stand in my way to fame and fortune. I was full-on bought into the world's definition of beauty and was willing to bleed to get there. Only now, I was conflicted by learning that Jesus was full-on bought into His Father's definition of beauty and was willing to bleed to get me there.

Now, I'm not making a blanket statement addressing all plastic surgery, but in my case, deep down, I did think that this completely elective, vain attempt at stardom was equivalent to telling God, "I don't like how You made me, buddy, and I am going to change some things around." This was a prideful attempt to be like God, which is much like the sin of pride that started the mess in the Garden of Eden in the first place.

Armed with a Discover Card that happened to show up in the mail, and a huge lack of discernment, I looked up some plastic surgeons from the phone book, closed my eyes, pointed to one, and decided I needed to make this thing happen. Still living at home, I somehow convinced my parents not to worry about me going under the knife, and I was convinced that this was going to advance my career and boost my self-esteem. After wrapping up finals and walking the stage to receive my college degree, I was ready to get in the ring of vanity and excess, to fight the Joneses for the prize of a glamorous payday, and yell, "Cut me, Mick," like Rocky, desperate to stay in the bout.

Scars from a Fake ID

Before that day, I'd had one consultation with the plastic surgeon, who had me feeling great about what the end result would be. I didn't want a big change, just enough. I explained that my ears in general were okay; it was just the earlobes in proportion to the ear. I figured we were on the same page of "just taking a little off the top." Then came the moment, like in the movies when an alien spaceship comes barreling down the street and the only words the unsuspecting guy in the street can say are "Oh, crap" before getting obliterated.

There I was, waking up in a fog from being under anesthesia on the operating-room table, but coherent enough to respond to the doctor with a yes when he asked if I wanted to see his handiwork. It's like when the barber hands you a mirror to see the back of your hair, only more permanent. As he unwrapped what was like a mummy cloth around my head, I was anxiously ready to see my perfect earlobes. When I gazed into the mirror expectantly, my heart sank to the floor and splattered on the ground. Homeboy hadn't even touched my earlobes! They were exactly the same. Come on! The Discover Card was maxed, and this was a onetime shot.

I was immediately humbled, even before I got off the table. I knew, lying on my back, that my decision to change something on the outside had everything to do with what I believed about myself on the inside. I really couldn't blame the doctor; besides, I'm pretty sure I signed a waiver that said I'd have to live with the results. He basically performed the bilateral otoplasty that he knew how to do, a surgery that sort of just repositioned the entire ear but didn't change the ear. For the next several years, I was actually even more self-conscious, because now, in addition to the thing I wanted to change the most in the front, I also had to worry about hiding the scars that were ever so present in the back.

Regardless of whether you can relate to the specifics of my experience, we probably share a desire to achieve the admiration of our peers and end the debate at the hairdresser. I wanted to be known as "Leading Man" no matter the cost. Others desire the labels "Perfect Mom," "Mr. Right," "Animal Lover," "Woke," "Ms. Successful," "Tech Guru," "TikTok Star," or some other title. Problems arise, though, when these otherwise good desires become the ultimate way we see ourselves. Where we find our truest identity determines much about the story we will write with our lives and the Grace Bombing adventures we may or may not have.

True Identity

At twenty-two, I figuratively carried a fake ID. I wanted to be seen as and feel like a model. I wanted to be known as an actor. I wanted to achieve the admiration of my peers. I believed I knew best. But as much as it feels like we should tell ourselves who we are, or allow our peers to define us, wouldn't it make the most sense to allow God to tell us who we are? And if what He says is true, wouldn't that impact so many of the decisions we'll make?

It took me several years to begin to embrace my identity as a grace-built person and to allow that true identity to drive me. The truth is that when it comes to who we really are—as opposed to what we might think or what our peers say—we are sitting on a treasure chest of life-giving grace that some of us have never opened up. In fact, God has unleashed a fury of heavenly Grace Bombs on each individual believer. The results of this are life-changing for us and for our neighbors, giving us unparalleled security and an unending fuel supply from which to energize all of our Grace Bombing efforts.

I'd like this final chapter to be a small Grace Bomb to you: a reminder Paul penned in Ephesians 1, based on one long sentence in the original Greek, about who you really are. If all this is true, you'll never need to tell God He didn't build you right ever again, and you'll have no need to break out fake IDs in order to impress people.

Dwell on these heavenly Grace Bombs in the assurance that they are absolutely true about you. Don't finish this chapter for information alone, but consider its truth for transformation. As my friend Jonathan likes to say, speak these things over your heart, even if they don't feel true right now.

What follows here is the true identity of grace-built people, and it is by grasping these realities and hanging on to them that you will be able to stop keeping up with the Joneses, instead being free to love them with no strings attached.

The apostle Paul started his long sentence about who you really are this way:

> Blessed be the God and Father of our Lord Jesus Christ, who has blessed us in Christ with every spiritual blessing in the heavenly places …
>
> Ephesians 1:3

There is something to be excited about in this verse that may not be immediately obvious. It is that these Grace Bombs are spiritual blessings kept for you in the heavenly places. In a world of instant gratification, and where seeing is believing, let me tell you why invisible realities are great news.

Many have been convinced, as I was for a long time, that material blessings are the best kind of blessings. Case in point, the Bugatti Chiron. I watched a documentary recently about hypercars. Hypercars, like the Bugatti, are the world's most technologically advanced, expensive, prestigious, and baller cars. These super automobiles are built like rocket ships on wheels, with price tags into the millions. I won't lie; I covet the hypercar. I'd gladly trade in the Gray Ghost (our minivan) for a hypercar. Wouldn't it be great to get grace bombed with a hypercar? Of course it would! I am not saying that material things are not blessings but that they are not the best blessing we should desire. There is an inherent problem with the objects we make with our hands: they fail to satisfy our hearts in the long run.

One of history's wealthiest people was King Solomon in the Old Testament, who was David's boy and the last king of the unified nation of ancient Israel. It was Solomon who ruled in a time of vast economic prosperity, and he was also rich with wisdom, telling us that "he who loves money will not be satisfied with money, nor he who loves wealth with his income; this also is vanity" (Eccl. 5:10). This word from the wise is aptly followed by the reason we won't be satisfied: "When goods increase, they increase who eat them, and what advantage has their owner but to see them with his eyes?" (v. 11). Solomon's point was that, as money, material blessings, and bling capture the affections of our hearts, our appetites grow along with our consumption, leaving us hungry for even more.

In other words, the Bugatti would be absolutely fun to drive for a while, but at some point, even the thrill of zero to sixty in under three seconds would get old, and we'd wonder what was next up for Bugatti. Maybe we'd trade up, or try the Porsche or Tesla. Apply this to anything you'd personally want to buy today. Tomorrow, there might be a better one. The reason we are left wanting more material blessings is because our souls want *more than* material blessings. They were made to be quenched by spiritual blessings, which is the very thing God provides first and foremost, and in abundance by a relationship with Him in Christ.

The reason we are left wanting more
material blessings is because our souls
want *more than* material blessings.

In Christ is an interesting phrase that requires some definition to even understand. This would be an odd thing to slap on a name tag and wear around: "Hi, I'm in Christ." So Paul's sentence continues with additional depth on what it means to be a grace-built person who has an endless supply of grace to draw from in Christ.

> … even as he chose us in him before the foundation of the world, that we should be holy and blameless before him.
>
> Ephesians 1:4

Grace-built people were chosen by God before the foundation of the world. This is what theologians call the "doctrine of election." Back in seminary in Columbia, South Carolina, I had two smart professors who both loved Jesus but had contrasting viewpoints about this mysterious and seemingly paradoxical concept of election. They were divided over the question "Do we choose God, or does He choose us?"

Much ink has been spilled on this topic by scholars and students of the Bible, and I don't intend to dive into the discussion here. But one thing to note is that Jesus expressed both concepts of divine sovereignty and human responsibility when He taught about people's eternal destinies.[2] In John's gospel, Jesus explained that God the Father must pave the way for people to believe, but also, each person has a real decision point whether or not to believe.

While it can be easy to get overly focused on the seemingly important question "Does God choose us, or do we choose Him?" let me point out what we might miss when we start that discussion. It's what the rest of the Ephesians verse indicates: the mind-blowing truth that God had plans for you before you were even born. Before the earth existed—when there was no time, space, or matter but only the self-existent, uncreated, and eternal spiritual Being, in perfect communal relationship between the Father, Son, and Holy Spirit—God was thinking about you, loving you, and intending for you to be set apart and holy like He is. He has seen your life, He has seen your death, He has known your heart, and He has superintended your journey to becoming a grace-built person when you were placed in Christ.

> He predestined us for adoption to himself as sons through Jesus Christ, according to the purpose of his will, to the praise of his glorious grace, with which he has blessed us in the Beloved.
>
> Ephesians 1:5–6

I often hear the phrase "We are all God's children," referring to all the people on planet Earth. This is an endearing idea, for sure, and I love the heart and gracious inclusion behind it. But if the

Bible is right here, then that phrase would be better spoken, "We are all God's *creation*." That still means that all people, regardless of any faith superstructure, have been created in God's image and are intrinsically valuable because of that very fact. But what Paul said was, to be a part of the relational family of God, we must be brought into that family, or in other words, adopted. To be a child of God, you must be brought in. One scholar remarked that the very word *adoption* refers to being placed as an adult son.[3]

Imagine for a minute that Sir Richard Branson of Virgin Records invites you out to his private island for a weekend. He flies you out on one of his jets, and instead of landing normally, you parachute out to the island just for the fun of it. Once there, you are allowed to stay in your own house and explore the island in your own off-road vehicle. During the stay, an extra ticket pops up for a private flight into outer space, now that Virgin Galactic is up and running. After your space lap, and a few more nights on the island, you return to your real life, thankful for the memories.

Now imagine the difference if when you get that call from Sir Richard, he also says he has found a legal way to adopt you, even though you're an adult. Although weird and unheard of, you are won over when he says that his stuff will be your stuff. The jet that picks you up, yours. The parachute, yours. The island, yours. The spacecraft, yours. The houses, yours. The business, yours. As a new member of the family, you are handed a set of keys.

Spiritually speaking, this is the great truth to which adoption points. As sons and daughters of God, we find ourselves with immediate access to God, all the comfort and confidence of being part of the family, and the ability to draw upon Him for all of our needs and to fulfill the deepest longings of our hearts. The greatest luxury is that we connect with God Himself, calling Him "Dad." After all, in teaching His disciples how to pray, Jesus led them to pray "our Father" (Matt. 6:9).

One of the best things about being a kid is the innocent assurance that your dad has got everything under control, so that you sleep well at night. Those were the good old days when our parents were invincible, and we could do anything, because they were the ultimate backstops in our lives. We were loved, before love got complicated, and we were free to run around naked, because we weren't trying to run the world.

Children with the luxury of a parent who loves and cares for them also have the luxury of feeling secure. And where there is security, there can be an openhandedness with our time and treasures used for grace bombing. When we escape self-preservation, leaving behind our demand that our needs are always met, we are more likely to tend to the needs of others.

There is a strong correlation between the love that we have received and the love that we are able to give. What if, deep down, all of us adults felt like little kids who could do anything because our parents ran the world? What if we stopped caring what other people thought because our identity was not coming from other people's likes or views, but from a loving parent who told us who we were? And what if that parent was absolutely right? How great it is to be a child at heart.

In chapter 1, I told you about Scarlett's desire to get her bomb on. About a month before that, she handed me this:

It was a simple, clear bag with a card, a love note, and 30 cents. When she gave it to me, she said, "This is for college." I don't know how her young mind arrived at that topic, but it warmed my heart. Much like what this parent shared on Instagram:

Oh, to be young and grace bomb the tooth fairy! Sometimes I wonder if God sees our Grace Bombs like we see Scarlett's and Harper's—these little sacrifices, from sweet and innocent children, that are pleasing to Him. Why wouldn't He be pleased? After all, we are His kids, and He has declared us innocent. That is the next part of our grace-built identity.

> In him we have redemption through his blood, the forgiveness of our trespasses, according to the riches of his grace, which he lavished upon us, in all wisdom and insight.
>
> Ephesians 1:7–8

The two heavenly Grace Bombs of redemption and forgiveness make the most sense in light of the fact that God is holy. God is utterly pure and morally perfect. He is the only truly set-apart and unique being. If *holy* is a word we use to describe the very nature of God, then the word commonly used to describe falling short of that holy perfection is *sin*. It means to miss the mark, like in archery, when the arrow doesn't hit the center. The word *trespass* is a similar idea, meaning to cross over a line that departs from God's holy standard. Sins and trespasses incur a spiritual debt to God that, because of His holy justice, must be reconciled.

When Paul said that we have been bombed with redemption, he was communicating in accounting terms that the sin debt was paid, the chains were loosed, and because Jesus paid the debt, we are set free. Before someone becomes grace-built, the Bible describes that person as being in bondage to sin, enslaved to it (Rom. 6:17). The idea of being free from sin is a liberating one, and this payment was made by Jesus who came "to give his life as a ransom for many" (Matt. 20:28). All of this is why, in Ephesians 1:7, "through his blood" sits next to "redemption"; the life of Jesus was the cost to buy back people from slavery to sin.

Redemption is closely related to the Grace Bomb of forgiveness. This heavenly blessing should make us feel differently about ourselves, as it speaks to the fact that our sins have been sent off or sent away. The removal of our guilt is particularly helpful for anyone who has a recurring track playing in their minds of how bad they have been and all the terrible things they have done.

God doesn't keep our sins on His mind. In repairing our relationship with Him, He put a great distance between us and all the bad things we've ever done (Ps. 103:12). There has been a complete removal, a full and final cleansing in Christ, for all the ways we fall short of God's holy standard—yesterday, today, and tomorrow. This is news that never gets old, because even though you might be following Jesus, there are bound to be times when you cave in to fear or temptation—or just lose sight of Him, on a crash course to the fresh need of grace all over again.

> In him we have obtained an inheritance, having been predestined according to the purpose of him who works all things according to the counsel of his will.
>
> Ephesians 1:11

This is what I call the Grace Bomb of a heavenly inheritance. When I think about an inheritance, my mind goes to all the equity, estates, and other material belongings that are passed down when family members distribute their material possessions through their wills. But far greater than money, the inheritance Paul was speaking of is an eternal relationship that continues after we die. Not many of us are looking forward to the prospect of death, but for the believer in Christ, "death is just a doorway to take [us] to our faithful lover."[4]

The believer can look forward to a face-to-face relationship with Jesus and experiencing unfiltered, uncorrupted love that can only be shared in *heaven*, where sin and its effects have no home. The apostle Peter was looking forward to this time when he wrote:

> According to his [God's] great mercy, he has caused
> us to be born again to a living hope through the

> resurrection of Jesus Christ from the dead, to an
> inheritance that is imperishable, undefiled, and
> unfading, kept in heaven for you. (1 Pet. 1:3–4)

This ex-fisherman captured pages' worth of theology in just two verses. First, he gave us the reason we have an amazing inheritance: God loves us, instead of immediately punishing us with what we deserve (great mercy), by giving us a regenerated spirit (born again) that provides us with a living hope (as opposed to a false or dead hope) based on the accomplishment of Jesus, all of which is verified in His resurrection. Then, Peter described this inheritance in three ways.

First, our inheritance is *imperishable*. This is a foreign concept for us because everything on earth is subject to death and decay. Eventually, the new car loses that new car smell, the shoes you wanted to keep pristine get scuffed, new songs get played out, and the invincible feelings of our youth give way to weird aches and pains that you can't even trace to an injury. Everything is winding down. But our life after death with Jesus is not subject to decay. It is life that never winds down, loses the new car smell, or gets scuffed, old, or achy because we haven't stretched the hamstrings in a while. An imperishable life is the kind of life God lives and gives, and the kind we get to look forward to. The way the Bible describes it, we won't be weird, disembodied souls, but we'll have new resurrected bodies—physical bodies, built to last for eternity in the presence of God (1 Cor. 15:42–44).

Second, our inheritance is *undefiled*. Peter was saying that our heavenly inheritance is pure, perfect, and free of corruption. This makes me think about creation, when Adam and Eve had a perfect and pure relationship with God—after they met each other for the first time and before their free will led them to walk away from God. This was a time of simplicity and purity in the relationship between God and man—a time of direct and personal communication, sharing, and love. This was also a time when adults experienced pure, childlike innocence. It was a picture of life as God intended, and our heavenly inheritance will be such a life.

And third, our inheritance is *unfading*. What a promise this is, since in this life we have only experienced fading. One of the few concepts I retained from college was "diminishing marginal utility," which is pretty much a fact of life. The excitement and rush of experiencing something new, whether a new book, a new song, or a new recipe, creates value in our lives for a while. But with every additional reading, hearing, or meal, the value that is added plateaus, then diminishes. We get used to things, and there is a fade factor.

This is not the case in the life to come with God in heaven. Getting to know God will never get faded, because enjoying life with God can never get old, as His creativity, beauty, and knowledge are boundless. And this characteristic of God's nature is probably why our relationships with other people are the most fade-resistant experiences we can have today. People, created in the image of God, are intended for relationship, discovery, and growth. It may be that your relationship with your favorite person today is just a small example of the unfading joy you will have with Jesus, who embodies our heavenly inheritance.

Not only do we get to look forward to spending boundless time with Jesus, but we can know that He is also excited about spending time with His people, the church. In John's gospel, before Jesus was betrayed and arrested, He prayed for His friends, the disciples, and those who would come after them. Jesus prayed comprehensively for those who would believe in Him, and eight times, in different forms, He referred to them as those "whom you [the Father] have given me [Jesus]" (John 17:2, 6, 9, 10, 11, 12, 24). Jesus described the gift that God the Father was giving Him as an inheritance of eternal relationships.

> In him you also, when you heard the word of truth, the gospel of your salvation, and believed in him, were sealed with the promised Holy Spirit, who is the guarantee of our inheritance until we acquire possession of it.
>
> Ephesians 1:13–14

On top of such hopeful expectation of the life to come, leave it to God to grace bomb us even further with a down payment on this heavenly inheritance that awaits us. The last blast of the fury of grace that shapes who we are is the person of the Holy Spirit.

Grace-built people are sealed, spiritually speaking, with the person of the Holy Spirit. A seal is something of an official declaration, a mark of authenticity, with a powerful agency backing it up. Being sealed with God the Holy Spirit, by the will of God the Father, because of God the Son, is quite reassuring. Even more, we can take our promise of heavenly inheritance to the bank because the down payment has been made.

This doesn't mean that we instantly are changed into people who will never mess up and always do everything right—but it does mean that, as far as eternity is concerned, we are untouchable. Jesus says, "I give them eternal life, and they will never perish, and no one will snatch them out of my hand. My Father, who has given them to me, is greater than all, and no one is able to snatch them out of the Father's hand" (John 10:28–29). If the Holy Spirit has been deposited, the rest of your inheritance is guaranteed.

As if the assurance of our salvation were not enough of a gift, we also learn from Jesus that the Holy Spirit is not only a reminder for tomorrow but also a Helper for today. God intends for us to grow as grace-built people, to mature, and to become more like Jesus— and the Holy Spirit's job is to help us with that. The Holy Spirit was active in carrying along and guiding the authors of the Bible (2 Pet. 1:21), and He is still active in helping us learn and apply those Scriptures to our lives (John 14:25–26). And as we have already seen, He regularly nudges us toward obedience to reach out and grace bomb our neighbors.

So what are we to make of these Grace Bombs that shape our true identity?

For starters, we rest in them. We receive them as gifts from a good Father. Tell your heart that this is who you truly are. Be filled with this love, care, and thoughtful concern for you. You are loved. Anchor your security and identity in this love, instead of in what the world tells you is beautiful. It is deep, thoughtful, providential, and practical. It is long-suffering and not going anywhere. It is a love to be experienced today. It is what our souls long for the most, the spiritual realities of being in a relationship with God. Enjoy these heavenly Grace Bombs. Enjoy Jesus and His freedom.

Remember too that these blessings are immeasurable. You can't count them up, and there are plenty to go around. These same

Grace Bombs that shape your identity are eagerly waiting to fall on another soon-to-be child of God. Your fuel supply today can become another's identity tomorrow, as your Grace Bombing adventures point them beyond mere kindness, to the source of kindness who is able to transform who they really are, scars and all.

So now, before you go and do, just be. Be that human being, created in the image of God, remade by God, and now in a relationship with God. This is why you were born, and this is the ultimate source of your identity. Life, friends, is a Grace Bomb. Enjoy it, so that your giving is an overflow of love, not an obligation of religion. Stay thankful and dependent on the Master Bomber, and then follow His invitation to drop grace on your neighbors with every surprising and soul-satisfying opportunity He provides.

Depth Charge

Heavenly Father:

- Thank You that You define me and tell me who I really am.
- Help me to see where I might be living with a fake ID, and empower me to rest in the riches of being Your child *in Christ*.
- Fill my mind with the heavenly reality that today I have all that I need, because I have You.
- Allow me to be vulnerable about my own scars, to the end that my neighbor can see the transforming power that You freely give.

Epilogue

Obedience is not a very popular word. It conjures up ideas of domineering leadership, the restriction of opportunity, or the elimination of freedoms. Well, it does for me anyway. Even as a kid, I shied away from obeying authority. Just ask all my teachers who sent me to the principal's office for insubordination, the handy catch-all term for when it was hard to pin me to a real crime. We are wise to be cautious about blindly following authority, because no person should have ultimate say in instructing and directing our lives.

Unless that person is God.

This is where obedience becomes a more intriguing opportunity. If Jesus truly is who He claimed to be—and if there really was a crucifixion followed by a literal and historical resurrection—then what must logically follow is that Jesus is the one person who has the right, and the wisdom, to call the shots in our lives. Who better to tell us how to live life than the inventor and sustainer of life itself?

Early in John's gospel we are confronted with this sentence: "All things were made through him, and without him was not any thing made that was made" (John 1:3). This means that Jesus was the agent of creation, the general contractor, if you will, to the grand blueprints of the Father. He forged the unfathomably large and intricately small space-time universe into reality from the unseen eternal spiritual dimension. He is the inventor of beauty, laughter, emotion, exhilaration, intimacy, learning, wisdom, language, gravity, love, and fun. God knows how it all works best, and He revealed Himself to take the guesswork out of who He is and what He desires.

God wants us to obey Him, because He knows that His will leads to the best possible outcomes of life. Those outcomes do not equate necessarily to our personal health, wealth, and happiness— but they do equate with carrying out our purpose in this life, which yields a soul-satisfying, regret-free, legacy-leaving joy. God doesn't want to just keep us out of trouble; He wants to equip us to join Him in rebuilding people with grace and truth.

Obedience is God's love language. Beyond what's in it for us, obedience to Jesus is how we tell Him "I love You back." Later in John's gospel, Jesus told His friends, "If you love me, you will keep my commandments" (14:15). For a big portion of my life, I told Jesus that I loved Him by going to a building with a cross on it, singing songs to Him and about Him, giving a little from time to time, surviving long-winded speakers, and largely keeping my faith in the confines of those four walls. The four walls are important, but God is calling us out to break the ice with our neighbors, and He is our ultimate motivation.

I am reminded here of the words of Oswald Chambers:

> A missionary is someone sent by Jesus Christ just as
> he was sent by God. The great controlling factor is
> not the needs of people, but the command of Jesus.
> The source of our inspiration in our service for God

is behind us, not ahead of us. The tendency today is to put the inspiration out in front—to sweep everything together in front of us and make it conform to our definition of success. But in the New Testament the inspiration is put behind us, and is the Lord Jesus Himself. The goal is to be true to Him—to carry out His plans.[1]

Grace Bomb is a movement of obedience to Jesus. Our marching orders are to love practically. Our targets are the people we bump into every day. Our weapons are built out of grace. Our icebreaker can be a simple card paired with surprising generosity. Our aim is the glory of God. And our great reward is not only spiritual growth but also simply telling Jesus, "I love You too."

Don't let the end of a book leave you in search of another book right away. Write your own story on the blank pages of tomorrow by your action in taking Jesus seriously today. And share the creative, fun, and surprising ways you are led to love your neighbor, to spur on all of us to love and good works! Tell me how it's going at gracebomb.org. Let's have some fun out there—it's time to fly.

Notes

Chapter 1: The Daddy-Daughter Date

1. "The Starfish Story" is a popular adaptation of an essay by Loren Eiseley called "The Star Thrower" in *The Unexpected Universe* (New York: Harcourt, Brace and World, 1969).

Chapter 2: Beyond #Kindness

1. See Romans 2:4 and Matthew 5:44–45.

2. The half man, half horse mythical creatures.

3. See Matthew 5:43–48; 7:12–14; John 13:34–35; and Luke 10:36–37.

Chapter 4: Grace-Built People

1. Robert Jamieson, A. R. Fausset, and David Brown, *Commentary Critical and Explanatory on the Whole Bible*, vol. 2 (Oak Harbor, WA: Logos Research Systems, Inc., 1997), 354.

2. See Mark 12:29–31; Matthew 22:34–40; Matthew 7:12; and Luke 6:31.

Chapter 6: The Outsiders

1. Warren W. Wiersbe, *The Bible Exposition Commentary*, vol. 1 (Wheaton, IL: Victor Books, 1996), 299.

2. R. A. Whitacre, *The IVP New Testament Commentary Series: John*, vol. 4 (Westmont, IL: IVP Academic, 1999), 101–2.

3. Wiersbe, *Bible Exposition*, 299.

Chapter 9: A New Love

1. "Baby's Got Sauce," track 5 on G. Love & Special Sauce, *G. Love & Special Sauce*, Epic Records, 1994.

2. For example, Nicodemus would have been familiar with Ezekiel 36:26–27, Jeremiah 24:7, Joel 2:28–29, or Deuteronomy 30:6.

3. The theological term for when God brings your soul alive to Him upon believing in Jesus.

Chapter 10: Fury Unleashed

1. "Blue steel" is a fashion-model move in the comedy film *Zoolander*.

2. See for example John 6:44 and John 8:2.

3. Warren W. Wiersbe, *The Bible Exposition Commentary*, vol. 1 (Wheaton, IL: Victor Books, 1996), 540.

4. "I'm Good," featuring Lecrae, track 3 on Trip Lee, *The Good Life*, Reach Records, 2012.

Epilogue

1. Oswald Chambers, *My Utmost for His Highest*, updated edition (Grand Rapids, MI: Discovery House, 1992), October 26.

BRING GRACE BOMB TO YOUR CHURCH

LOVE YOUR NEIGHBORS.

EQUIP YOUR CONGREGATION TO TAKE JESUS' COMMAND SERIOUSLY.

Grace Bomb is a practical bridge that answers "what's next" in between your church's organized community service events and mission trips. This decentralized and Spirit-led tool empowers "ordinary" people to become everyday missionaries, greatly multiplying the collective impact of each local church.

Unleash the untapped neighbor-loving potential in your congregation, and help them grow with in-depth sermons, small group discussion guides, media, and other discipleship resources that are **completely free** to churches.

GRACEBOMB.ORG/YOURCHURCH

LOAD. LISTEN. LET 'ER GO!

CARRY CARDS WITH YOU. PRAYERFULLY LISTEN FOR OPPORTUNITIES.
LOVE YOUR NEIGHBOR WITH A SURPRISING GIFT.

Start your Grace Bombing adventure using the cards in
this book, and order more cards at **gracebomb.org**.

BE INSPIRED.
INSPIRE OTHERS.

Follow Grace Bomb on social media to find
inspiring stories of everyday people loving
their neighbors, and share your story at
gracebomb.org to encourage others in their
Grace Bombing adventures!

GRACEBOMB.ORG • @GRACE.BOMB • FACEBOOK.COM/GRACEBOMBCO

And let us consider how to stir up one another to love and good works...
HEBREWS 10:24